IF YOU LOVE ME...

Kenneth D. Barney

**Gospel Publishing House
Springfield, Missouri**
02-0889

IF YOU LOVE ME . . .
© 1977 by the Gospel Publishing House
Springfield, Missouri 65802
This book is adapted from *Practical Christian Living* by Wildon Colbaugh, © 1963 by the Gospel Publishing House.

All rights reserved. No part of the text may be reproduced in any form without written permission of the publishers, except brief quotations used in connection with reviews in magazines or newspapers.
Library of Congress Catalog Card Number 75-22611
International Standard Book Number 0-88243-889-1
Printed in the United States of America

A teacher's guide for group study with this book is available from the Gospel Publishing House (order number 32-0163).

Contents

1 The Greatest of These 5

2 Forgive Us, as We Forgive 15

3 The Rebel Isn't Smart 24

4 It's the Best Policy 34

5 Stay in Command! 44

6 Keep Your Cool 54

7 It Helps Lighten the Load 63

8 There's Nothing Wrong With Humble Pie 73

9 Learn to Say "Thank You" 82

10 Old Faithful 91

11 Take Time to Be Holy 100

12 No Long Faces in This Crowd! 109

13 Peace Without Pills 118

1 COR 13:13

1 The Greatest of These

"The greatest of these is love," Paul declared. He was comparing faith, hope, and love (charity) in 1 Corinthians 13. Why is love the greatest? Because the day will come when we will not have to live by hope or faith. In heaven it will all be sight! But will love ever disappear? Never! Heaven will be saturated with it.

No matter what you're building you have to start with the foundation. Can we not call love the foundation of practical Christian living? Without it there is no Christian living at all. So we're putting first things first and talking about love and its effect on our relationship with God and each other.

With Everything in You

Doesn't it seem natural to think of our love for God first? If a man doesn't love God he can't really love his fellowman with the kind of love that is well-rounded and full. Let's listen to some very strong words of Jesus:

"And one of the scribes came, and having heard them reasoning together, and perceiving that he had answered them well, asked him, Which is the first commandment of all? And Jesus answered him, The first of all the commandments is, Hear O Israel;

The Lord our God is one Lord: and thou shalt love the Lord thy God with all thy heart, and with all thy soul, and with all thy mind, and with all thy strength: this is the first commandment" (Mark 12:28-30).

Those words bear repeating: "With all thy heart, and with all thy soul, and with all thy mind, and with all thy strength." In other words, love God with all that's in you. He must be the first object of a Christian's love—God himself.

It is unthinkable that we should not love the One who has redeemed us from our sins. Real love costs. God's love for us cost so much our mortal minds cannot comprehend it. But all He asks in return is our love and devotion. Jesus declared that "this is the first commandment." It takes priority over all else.

It is possible to speak of love in cold, mechanical terms. But look at everything our love for God is to take in: our heart, soul, mind, and strength—our whole being. This love is not to be passive, but wholehearted, warm, and intense. We are to love God with our emotions, our intellect, and even our physical powers. Everything we have and are must be placed at His disposal.

He Loved Us First

"He that loveth not, knoweth not God; for God is love. In this was manifested the love of God toward us, because that God sent his only begotten Son into the world, that we might live through him. Herein is love, not that we loved God, but that he loved us, and sent his Son to be the propitiation for our sins. . . . We love him, because he first loved us" (1 John 4:8-10,19).

That we should love God is not a startling statement. Why shouldn't we? But for God to love us—

that's a bit staggering. He started loving us when we were rebels against His laws. We had our backs to Him, but He loved us and kept trying to get our attention. His was a love that acted. He did more than just say, "I love you, world." He sent His Son into the world. He gave the best He had. There were barriers between us and Him, and He didn't want that. So He did something about it.

We often say this, but how deeply do we comprehend it: "God is love"? There are many other attributes of God—power, wisdom, authority—but somehow the attribute of love is the one that seems to reach down where we humans live.

The More You Know, the More You'll Love

"Hereby know we that we dwell in him, and he in us, because he hath given us of his Spirit. And we have seen and do testify that the Father sent the Son to be the Saviour of the world. Whosoever shall confess that Jesus is the Son of God, God dwelleth in him, and he in God. And we have known and believed the love that God hath to us. God is love; and he that dwelleth in love dwelleth in God, and God in him. Herein is our love made perfect, that we may have boldness in the day of judgment: because as he is, so are we in this world. There is no fear in love; but perfect love casteth out fear: because fear hath torment. He that feareth is not made perfect in love" (1 John 4:13-18).

Isn't knowledge the basis of love? Can you love someone you don't know? This is just as true in our relationship to God as it is to other humans. The more you know Him the more you'll love Him.

That's the thrilling thing about the Christian life. Each day brings an increase in our knowledge of the

Lord. This knowledge comes especially through reading the Bible and prayer. That's why it's so important to establish these practices and keep them diligently. It's worth the effort—a thousand times over.

What You Give, You'll Get Back

"And the second is like, namely this, Thou shalt love thy neighbor as thyself. There is none other commandment greater than these. And the scribe said unto him, Well, Master, thou hast said the truth: for there is one God; and there is none other but he: and to love him with all the heart, and with all the understanding, and with all the soul, and with all the strength, and to love his neighbor as himself, is more than all whole burnt offerings and sacrifices. And when Jesus saw that he answered discreetly, he said unto him, Thou are not far from the kingdom of God. And no man after that durst ask him any question" (Mark 12:31-34).

The scribe who was talking to Jesus had more than most of his fellows when it came to spiritual discernment. God must have been dealing with him. His answer seems sincere. It had dawned on him that all of the sacrifices and offerings of Old Testament worship were empty if not coupled with love.

The commandment to love our neighbor is second only to the commandment to love God. In His Parable of the Good Samaritan Jesus made it clear that anyone in need is our neighbor. It matters not what nationality or race he is. Compassion knows no barriers.

Our lives involve constant contact with others. There is no way to run and hide. The worldly man has little time for others. His main concern is "Number One." This is completely contrary to the Spirit of

Christ and must have no place in the lives of Christians. Above all, the believer must be known to everyone as one who cares.

Love does not demand perfection. It tolerates shortcomings and mistakes. It is not harsh in its judgment. It makes allowances for weaknesses. Love doesn't intentionally hurt anyone. On the contrary, the one filled with love will bend over backward to *avoid* hurting someone.

The unkind word, the slur, the cutting remark —none of these are in the vocabulary of love. Love does not easily take offense. It overlooks ill-treatment and unkindness on the part of others. And don't forget Paul's statement in 1 Corinthians 13:5 that love does not "behave itself unseemly." Love refines the nature and character. It eliminates coarseness and vulgarity.

And remember this: Love begets love. If you show love, you'll get love back. The more you show, the more you'll receive in return. This is a divine principle and it works.

It's God's Command

Does God say, "Love is a good thing. I would appreciate it if you could see your way clear to show it once in a while"? Hardly. He makes it a command. Here are some choice verses:

"Beloved, let us love one another: for love is of God; and everyone that loveth is born of God, and knoweth God. . . . Beloved, if God so loved us, we ought also to love one another. No man hath seen God at any time. If we love one another, God dwelleth in us, and his love is perfected in us. . . . If a man say, I love God, and hateth his brother, he is a liar: for he that loveth not his brother whom he hath seen, how can he love God whom he hath not seen? And this commandment have we from him, That he who loveth God love his brother also" (1 John 4:7,11, 12,20,21).

So much selfishness, greed, hate, violence, disloyalty, and betrayal exists in so-called Christian lands that it may sometimes appear that the virtue of love is altogether lost. The Christian must not allow the spirit of the age to crowd the spirit of love out of his heart. The fact still remains that "God is love." With this great ideal before us we can still be filled with love in a world of hate. There is no greater testimony to the power of the gospel.

If love is of God, then the closer we live to God the more love we will show. This may sound trite, but sometimes we need to reemphasize the simple truths. Communion with God is the only way to keep the fire of love aglow.

John appeals to us on the basis of God's love for us. If God is able to overlook the many things in *us* that aren't good, surely we can do the same for each other. John says that although no one has ever seen God, God is brought a little closer to us when love is displayed.

John is known as the "apostle of love," but he gets pretty sharp with his language here. He declares that a man is a liar if he professes to love God but hates his brother. His reasoning is logical: If you can't love someone you can see, how can you love One you *can't* see? A sobering question, isn't it? It's one we ought to ask ourselves the next time we are tempted to let hatred fester in our heart, or when that unforgiving spirit rears its ugly head!

It's a commandment, John says. He had heard Jesus himself command His small circle of disciples to love one another. He remembered that Jesus said this would be the way the world would recognize them as His disciples. It was a lesson John never forgot.

The Real Test

"Ye have heard that it hath been said, Thou shalt love thy neighbor, and hate thine enemy. But I say unto you, Love your enemies, bless them that curse you, do good to them that hate you, and pray for them which despitefully use you, and persecute you; that ye may be the children of your Father which is in heaven: for he maketh his sun to rise on the evil and on the good, and sendeth rain on the just and on the unjust. For if ye love them which love you, what reward have ye? do not even the publicans the same? And if ye salute your brethren only, what do ye more than others? do not even the publicans so? Be ye therefore perfect, even as your Father which is in heaven is perfect" (Matthew 5:43-48).

Love our friends—that's not too hard. Love our family—that's no problem. Love our enemies—there's the test. It really puts the finger on our character. It's like shining a big spotlight on the inside of us.

Jesus himself declared that to love the lovable is no great accomplishment. Neither is it an evidence of Christianity to love those who treat us well. To love those who misuse us and do not care for us is the acid test. It can be accomplished only with God's help. It's not a mechanical thing. Such love must originate deep within us.

Will a Christian have enemies? Strangely enough, yes. The very fact that he *is* a Christian will make some people his enemies. They feel uncomfortable around someone who lives by righteous standards.

Such a life is a rebuke to them. It turns a spotlight on their own sinfulness.

All the things Jesus told us to do toward our enemies are exactly the opposite of the natural human reaction. To love them, bless them, do good to them, and pray for them is not the way of the world. Yet Jesus said it is the thing that will mark us as His followers. The world will sit up and take notice when they see someone with such an attitude. They may shake their heads and wonder what makes him tick but they can't ignore him.

The path of least resistance is to throw up our hands in defeat and cry, "It can't be done." Some have said lamely, "I'll forgive, but I can't forget." When there is no forgetting, there is actually no forgiving. So we can't get by with this kind of cop-out.

If this kind of life weren't possible God wouldn't have commanded it. It is hard, but it is not unattainable. The question is: How badly do we *want* to love our enemies?

Jesus Showed Us How

As in all things, Jesus himself is our great Example. He never did anything but good, yet no one was ever so severely hated. What was His answer to this hatred? It was: "Father, forgive them; for they know not what they do" (Luke 23:34).

Jesus realized that hatred only begets more hatred. Anger begets more anger. Harsh words and retaliation only keep the same thing going in an endless cycle. Each time there is retaliation it must be more severe than the last time. Eventually things can build up to a big explosion.

You have heard the old adage about "killing with kindness." There is a lot of truth in it. If you have an enemy who is pouring it on you hot and heavy, try the kindness treatment. It will disarm him, throw him off balance, and make him feel foolish. It is very hard to keep fighting someone who is only giving you smiles and kind words in return. Eventually the enemy runs out of ammunition.

Jesus said that if the Father only treated people well who love and serve Him a lot of folks would never get any sunshine or rain. God would bypass them with both just to punish them for their ill-treatment of Him. But when He sends sunshine He lets it beam down on the sinner as well as the saint. When He sends rain it soaks the atheist's field as well as the Christian's.

Jesus taught His followers to turn the other cheek instead of slugging the one who lets us have it. No one demonstrated this more than He. When He was taken in Gethsemane He could have killed all His opponents with a word, but He didn't. When Peter cut an ear off one of them, Jesus healed it. He warned the apostle that he who takes up the sword will perish with the sword. This means that if you use the world's weapons you'll eventually be destroyed yourself.

The one who follows Jesus in His treatment of enemies may often be ridiculed. Friends may cry, "You let everyone walk all over you." It is sorely tempting to heed them and go all out in revenge. But such a temptation should be resisted. In the end it will only breed more trouble. It will hurt one's Christian testimony. Leave the "getting even" to the Lord. Commit your case to Him. In the end He'll handle it a whole lot better than you can. Wouldn't it be a miracle if you turned an enemy into a friend?

We're talking about one of the greatest challenges in the Christian life. It takes prayer, dedication, and real determination. Above all, it takes the grace of God. And that grace will be there when you need it.

Don't Forget the Sinner

Before we found Christ we were all sinners. Aren't you glad there were Christians that loved us and helped us find salvation? Let's never forget what we once were. It's a bad thing to become so secure in our own salvation that we forget others still on the outside.

Here again our love for God is the starting point. If we love Him we will surely feel His love for the lost. If our love for the Lord cools, so will our concern for the unsaved.

God didn't wait until we got better to make plans to save us. He started while we were still far from Him. God has placed within our hands the power to influence the lives of the unconverted. He doesn't use angels to bring them to himself. He uses redeemed sinners. Who knows how many we may bring into the fold if we will let the Lord use us.

Obviously we must be careful of the life we live before the unsaved. Example is a powerful testimony. And when we get a chance to say something we should never let the opportunity slip. That lost friend may be just waiting for a word of encouragement from you. It could be the thing that turns him toward the Lord. Let Christ's love shine through you!

1 COR. 13:4

2 Forgive Us, As We Forgive

We have just finished talking about love. Now here's a subject that's closely related—*forgiveness*. It's another test of Christian character. There is no way to talk about practical Christian living without discussing forgiveness.

The dictionary defines *forgive* very simply: "To pardon, as a sin or offense; to remit, as a debt." When a pardon is issued to someone guilty of a crime he is freed from further punishment. The state no longer holds the offense against him. When a debt is forgiven it is canceled. The creditor no longer expects payment. This gives us a pretty fair idea of what our attitude should be toward those we forgive.

It's God's Command

"And forgive us our debts, as we forgive our debtors. And lead us not into temptation, but deliver us from evil: For thine is the kingdom, and the power, and the glory, for ever. Amen. For if ye forgive men their trespasses, your heavenly Father will also forgive you: but if ye forgive not men their trespasses, neither will your Father forgive your trespasses" (Matthew 6:12-15).

Forgiveness is one of God's great attributes, and it is His will that it become a part of our lives. In fact,

God places a demand on everyone who comes to Him in prayer. If we wish to be accepted and heard by Him we must have a forgiving heart. Jesus makes it very strong when He says that if we won't forgive others God won't forgive us. So forgiving others is not an option.

Mark records the same command, although he words it a little differently: "And when ye stand praying, forgive, if ye have aught against any; that your Father also which is in heaven may forgive you your trespasses. But if ye do not forgive, neither will your Father which is in Heaven forgive your trespasses (Mark 11:25,26).

Solemn words like these ought to make us think twice when we feel we can't forgive. Our relationship with God is deeply involved. He is a Forgiver, and we can't be like Him if we don't treat others the same way.

Notice how Jesus connects this forgiving attitude with our prayer life: "When ye stand praying, forgive." The next time we pray let's examine our hearts and make sure there are no grudges or hard feelings there. If there are, we must deal with them immediately.

You're Only Hurting Yourself

The one who will not forgive is hurting one person most of all—himself. He will soon discover that it is a great hindrance in his spiritual development. He will find it difficult to pray. Invariably the Holy Spirit will bring the matter to his mind, and if he does not get the victory he will find his communion with the Lord stifled.

An unforgiving spirit is somewhat like a cancer. The longer it is allowed to remain, the larger it grows.

It produces bitterness and harshness. It saps the joy and victory from life.

We should remember that there may be a time when we too will need to be forgiven by someone else. As we sow we shall also reap. If we are not willing to forgive there will probably be those who will not forgive us. A harsh spirit produces more harshness in return.

"Two wrongs do not make a right." Our refusal to forgive does not correct any situation—it makes it far worse. If we do not forgive, we too are in the wrong. We drive the other person farther from us.

Nothing gives sweeter relief than erasing hard feelings and freely forgiving someone who has wronged us. It will help him, too. Very likely he will not repeat the wrong if he knows we have freely forgiven him. If he does repeat it the responsibility is on his shoulders, not ours. We have done the Christlike thing in forgiving. Our consciences are clear and our spiritual life is enhanced.

Here's a good verse: "And be ye kind one to another, tenderhearted, forgiving one another, even as God for Christ's sake hath forgiven you" (Ephesians 4:32). Remember that Paul is writing to Christians. Does this mean that there are times when one Christian must forgive another? Yes, we're human and sometimes conflicts arise even between God's children. The manner in which we handle such matters has a great bearing on our character. It also has an influence on the church. It is possible for the spiritual progress of a whole congregation to be stymied because of individual members who won't forgive each other.

Refusing to forgive is a form of mental revenge. Maybe we won't do physical harm to the other fellow, but in our minds we are constantly striking out at him. It makes the carnal nature feel good sometimes, but it is devastating to the spiritual nature. It certainly doesn't make the Holy Spirit feel at home. In fact, it grieves Him. He cannot dwell where there is a spirit full of bitterness.

Forgive Who?

"But love ye your enemies, and do good, and lend, hoping for nothing again; and your reward shall be great, and ye shall be the children of the Highest: for he is kind unto the unthankful and to the evil. Be ye therefore merciful, as your Father also is merciful. Judge not, and ye shall not be judged: condemn not, and ye shall not be condemned: forgive, and ye shall be forgiven" (Luke 6:35-37).

Trespassers

To live in this world without suffering wrong of some kind is wishful thinking. Hardly a day passes that we are not subjected to the wrongdoings of someone. The Bible sometimes calls such wrongs "trespasses."

The trespasser is not always one who hurts us willfully. He may be unaware of what he has done. On the other hand, his deed may be intentional. In any case, we must forgive those who trespass against us. The wrong may be severe. We may not understand why God has allowed it. But if God has forgiven our trespasses we must forgive those done against us.

Look at Joseph. Imagine having your own brothers sell you into slavery. For years Joseph was separated from home and family. It was not for any wrong he had done. The whole dastardly situation grew out of hatred and jealousy on the part of his brothers. Did

Joseph brood over the wrong and let bitterness overwhelm him? Fortunately he knew God well enough to overcome his feelings. There is no more beautiful story in the Bible than the account of Joseph's forgiveness of his brothers.

David suffered terrible wrong at the hands of Saul. Again, jealousy was the motive. Saul's hatred grew so violent that David was driven into exile. Yet when he had opportunity to kill Saul he refused. In the long run, who won? David, of course. He became king in God's time, while Saul died a miserable death and undoubtedly lost his soul.

Persecutors

"Bless them which persecute you: bless, and curse not. . . . Recompense to no man evil for evil. . . . Dearly beloved, avenge not yourselves, but rather give place unto wrath: for it is written, Vengeance is mine; I will repay, saith the Lord. Therefore if thine enemy hunger, feed him; if he thirst, give him drink: for in so doing thou shalt heap coals of fire on his head. Be not overcome of evil, but overcome evil with good" (Romans 12:14,17,19-21).

A persecutor is one who actively harasses. There have been times in church history when this has been violent. Christians have been tortured, imprisoned, and even martyred. In our own land we are not likely to suffer like this. Yet there is often deliberate annoyance, opposition, vexation, and even hatred toward the Christian. Such intentional opposition is usually harder to forgive, but we must pray for the grace to do it.

The first Christian martyr was Stephen. While his persecutors rained stones on him he prayed, "Lord, lay not this sin to their charge" (Acts 7:60). Certainly he displayed the spirit of his Lord in that tragic hour. Such forgiveness is a grace imparted to the character by the indwelling of the Holy Spirit.

Our persecution is often the subtle kind. We may face the power of snobbery and class distinction. Cliques on the job, in school, and in the neighborhood can let the Christian know in no uncertain terms that he is an outsider. What really hurts is when persecution comes from one's own family. It often does, and this is part of the price of discipleship. It may be harder to forgive a relative than someone else. Their jabs may have more sting. But forgiveness and kindness will do far more to win them than retaliation. It will also develop our Christian character.

Enemies

"Love your enemies, bless them that curse you, do good to them that hate you, and pray for them which despitefully use you, and persecute you" (Matthew 5:44).

There are those who are such out-and-out opponents that the word *enemy* is the only one that fits. There seems to be no common ground on which we can compromise with them. It is a complete stand-off. There is no give, no flexibility; only enmity.

How can we forgive our enemies? We need God's help. Don't forget that we were once His enemies and He forgave us. The Bible teaches that we are to go out of our way to do deeds of kindness to our enemies. If the barriers can be broken down, this will do it. Hostility will not.

Enemies are often filled with hate. We cannot return this hate. We *must* not. Such people may even attack our reputation and character. They may try to turn our friends against us. Never forget Jesus faced such people constantly. He said if we encounter these situations we are to forgive. Ill feelings must be eradicated; prayed out. They are never to be held and nurtured.

How Much?

Sometimes folks are willing to forgive a little, but their forgiveness has a limit. Maybe once or twice, but after that—look out!

Matthew 18:15-35 deals with the problem of forgiveness at some length. In verses 15-17 Jesus said:

"Moreover if thy brother shall trespass against thee, go and tell him his fault between thee and him alone: if he shall hear thee, thou has gained thy brother. But if he will not hear thee, then take with thee one or two more, that in the mouth of two or three witnesses every word may be established. And if he shall neglect to hear them, tell it unto the church: but if he neglect to hear the church, let him be unto thee as a heathen man and a publican."

Our Saviour gave a very clear procedure here. There may be extreme instances where the offender is so depraved that he won't even listen to the church, but usually this is not the case. Note that the main emphasis of Jesus is on winning back the friendship of the trespasser: "If he shall hear thee, thou hast gained thy brother." This is the main thing we should strive for.

This seemed to raise a question in Peter's mind. Here's how his conversation with Jesus went:

"Then came Peter to him, and said, Lord, how oft shall my brother sin against me, and I forgive him? till seven times? Jesus saith unto him, I say not unto thee, Until seven times: but, Until seventy times seven" (vv. 21,22).

Obviously Jesus did not mean that after 490 times we should stop forgiving. He was stressing the unlimited forgiveness that should characterize a Christian.

To reinforce His lesson Jesus gave a parable (Matthew 18:23-35). He talked about a king who was going to sell a man and his family into slavery for the payment of a debt. Since the man didn't have enough money the only thing he could do was throw himself on the king's mercy. Verse 27 beautifully states: "Then the lord of that servant was moved with compassion, and loosed him, and forgave him the debt."

But that wasn't the end of the story. The man who had just had his debt canceled found someone who owed him a small amount and threw him into prison. When the king heard the news he withdrew the cancelation of the man's debt to him and angrily jailed him. Jesus ended the story with a solemn warning: "So likewise shall my heavenly Father do also unto you, if ye from your hearts forgive not every one his brother their trespasses" (v. 35).

It's Not Impossible

This attitude of complete forgiveness is not an unattainable goal. It will take prayer, diligent study of the Word, and the help of the Holy Spirit. But it will be worth it all to know we are following in the steps of the Master.

It is easy for our forgiveness to be superficial—from the teeth out. Real forgiveness comes from the *heart*.

The System Bible Study offers this choice bit of advice concerning forgiveness: "Be charitable. Remember that all temperaments are not the same, nor are all the circumstances which surround people the same in every case. Make allowance for temper, training, nationality, education (or lack of it), and circumstances. Under the right influences we have seen weak people become strong, sour people become sweet, and ill-tempered people become sane and reasonable. Remember, too, that many men are better than they appear. Richard Baxter, after the closest contact with the severest Puritans of the Commonwealth, and the most licentious cavaliers of the Restoration, writes in his old age: 'I see that good men are not so good as I once thought they were, and find that few men are as bad as their enemies imagine.'"

It will help us to study and restudy the life of Jesus in the Gospels. Observe His reaction to those who constantly maligned, ridiculed, hated, and persecuted Him even to the death. From the cross itself He cried, "Father, forgive them; for they know not what they do" (Luke 23:34).

What Jesus is we can become. This is not through any power or goodness of our own, but through His help. The world desperately needs the spirit of forgiveness, mercy, and long-suffering. It can only see it if we live it.

Here is a beautiful passage from Colossians 3:12, 13: "Put on therefore, as the elect of God, holy and beloved, bowels of mercies, kindness, humbleness of mind, meekness, long-suffering; forbearing one another, and forgiving one another, if any man have a quarrel against any: even as Christ forgave you, so also do ye."

We're thankful that Christ forgave us, aren't we? Do we imagine that anyone can wrong us more than we wronged Him? Then let's show His spirit in dealing with those who don't treat us right.

3 The Rebel Isn't Smart

Everyone knows the whole universe operates by laws. Who would be foolish enough to jump off a skyscraper and dare the law of gravity to make him crash? The stars and planets move in split-second precision because their movements are governed by laws. What if it were possible for those bodies to defy the laws and make up their own? There would soon be a crash that would wipe out everything.

It is time we learned there are spiritual laws as well as physical laws. Our obedience to them is just as vital as the obedience of the heavenly bodies to physical laws.

Authority Starts With God

In recent years we have seen a wave of rebellion against everything. All that has ever existed is categorized as the "establishment." Some think it is all bad, and they want to wipe it out. The spirit of anarchy has reared its ugly head and accomplished nothing but chaos.

This widespread rebellion often affects people's relationship to God. They want to forget His laws and make up their own. Children want to defy parents. Students delight in flouting the rules of the school.

Police are the targets of hate. Anything that stands for authority is downgraded and despised.

Some imagine that respect for authority is a sign of weakness. Most certainly it is not. Without obedience we have only anarchy and strife. And our own personalities become warped. Why? Because God himself is the Author of law and authority. To defy Him is to destroy one's self.

In the Biblical account of Creation it is continually recorded, "And God said." God spoke, and the elements obeyed His voice. When God created man He had rules for him to obey. It was when man disobeyed that sin entered the world. With it came sickness, death, and the turmoil that has so often engulfed the human race.

Our reaction to the laws of God underlies all our actions toward other people. If we obey God we will be able to live in harmony with the laws of the home, church, state, and nation. If we disobey Him we will be at odds with everyone and everything around us. A person who flaunts God's laws will do the same with man's laws. Rebellion is an attitude of the spirit.

The Bible Is Our Guide

The supreme law of this universe is God's law, revealed through His Word. The first concise formulation of God's moral law was in the Ten Commandments given to Moses. These are so important that we take the time to repeat them here:

(1) Thou shalt have no other gods before me.

(2) Thou shalt not make unto thee any graven image.

(3) Thou shalt not take the name of the Lord thy God in vain.

(4) Remember the Sabbath Day, to keep it holy.

(5) Honor thy father and thy mother.
(6) Thou shalt not kill.
(7) Thou shalt not commit adultery.
(8) Thou shalt not steal.
(9) Thou shalt not bear false witness.
(10) Thou shalt not covet (Exodus 20:3-17).

Of course, there are many commandments of the Lord throughout the Bible. But what we call the Ten Commandments summarize the requirements God put on the human race. Every Christian society in the world has this great moral law as its basis.

Deuteronomy 5:32,33 is an Old Testament passage, but it states a divine principle that never changes: "Ye shall observe to do therefore as the Lord your God hath commanded you: ye shall not turn aside to the right hand or to the left. Ye shall walk in all the ways which the Lord your God hath commanded you, that ye may live, and that it may be well with you, and that ye may prolong your days in the land which ye shall possess."

Some may argue that it is impossible to live in a world like ours and obey God's Word. This would be true if we tried to do it in our own strength. But the Holy Spirit is given to believers to enable them to understand God's laws and keep them.

In John 14:15 Jesus said: "If ye love me, keep my commandments." Then He immediately declared: "And I will pray the Father, and he shall give you another Comforter, that he may abide with you for ever." After telling His disciples that the Spirit would actually dwell *in* them (v. 17), Jesus said: "He that hath my commandments, and keepeth them, he it is that loveth me" (v. 21).

It is evident that He connected the indwelling of the Spirit with the keeping of His commandments.

Basically, the Spirit makes us *want* to keep them. He gives us an understanding of them as we read the Bible. He makes clear the divine laws that would otherwise puzzle us.

There is a passage in the Book of James that emphasizes the importance of reading the Word every day to keep ourselves in line with God's laws:

"But be ye doers of the word, and not hearers only, deceiving your own selves. For if any be a hearer of the word, and not a doer, he is like unto a man beholding his natural face in a glass: for he beholdeth himself, and goeth his way, and straightway forgetteth what manner of man he was. But whoso looketh into the perfect law of liberty, and continueth therein, he being not a forgetful hearer, but a doer of the work, this man shall be blessed in his deed" (1:22-25).

A Solid Foundation

A house is no better than its foundation. So it is with a life. Obedience to God builds stability into the life and character. Jesus illustrated this forcefully with a well-known parable:

"Why call ye me, Lord, Lord, and do not the things which I say? Whosoever cometh to me, and heareth my sayings, and doeth them, I will show you to whom he is like: he is like a man which built a house, and digged deep, and laid the foundation on a rock: and when the flood arose, the stream beat vehemently upon that house, and could not shake it; for it was founded upon a rock" (Luke 6:46-48).

When we put into practice the instructions in God's Word it soon becomes evident to everyone that we have developed a strong character. We will be stable and reliable.

Then there is this statement in 1 John 5:3: "For this is the love of God, that we keep his commandments." In other words, love for the Lord shows itself in our obedience to His Word. How else would people know that we love Him?

A spirit of submission to the Lord will make us master of situations in life that might otherwise defeat us. An attitude of rebellion and stubbornness destroys our power of resistance to the attacks of Satan.

If we do not make God's will our final authority we will invariably make our own will the authority. This is one of the weaknesses of society today. There are too many wills battling against each other. No one wants to submit; everyone wants his own way. Such a spirit has no place in the life of a Christian.

No matter what realm of life you consider, someone has to give the orders and someone has to obey. This is true in business. It is true in school. Motorists have to obey traffic signals for the safety of everyone. For someone to say, "I don't have to obey," is a gross display of weak character. Plain intelligence tells us there has to be submission to authority. A Christian should set the example in this.

Obeying Other Humans

Obeying God may not be so hard, but some folks have a terrible time submitting to other humans. However, being obedient to God shapes our attitude toward human authority. Human government was established by the Lord himself. This doesn't mean everyone in authority is perfect. We don't obey because of perfection. We obey because God tells us we must. One who knowingly breaks God's laws will break man's also. Keeping God's laws makes it much easier to keep man's laws.

Deuteronomy 28:1-14 is another Old Testament passage that lays down divine principles that are still true. In the first verse God promised: "And it shall come to pass, if thou shalt hearken diligently unto the voice of the Lord thy God, to observe and to do all his commandments which I command thee this day, that the Lord thy God will set thee on high above all nations of the earth." The rest of the passage tells the kind of blessings that will come as a result of obedience.

The basis of society is the home. So God has given authority to the home. We are commanded to honor our father and mother. This admonition is repeated in the New Testament. In Ephesians 6:1 Paul says: "Children, obey your parents in the Lord: for this is right."

God intended that during the early, formative years of life we should learn to obey a law higher than our own will. Children accustomed to obeying their parents are more agreeable than those who are not. Obedience has a healthy effect on one's character and personality. This is true of older folks as well as children.

The uninhibited nature of man would assert itself without restraint if allowed to do so. Obedience does not come naturally, but through training. Parents must realize that they are not doing their children a favor by refusing to discipline them. If obedience isn't learned in the home, where *will* it be learned?

Here's another potent passage: "Wives, submit yourselves unto your own husbands, as it is fit in the Lord. Husbands, love your wives, and be not bitter against them. Children, obey your parents in all things: for this is well pleasing unto the Lord. Fathers, provoke not your children to anger, lest they be discouraged. Servants, obey in all things your masters according to the flesh; not with eyeservice, as menpleasers; but in singleness of heart, fearing God" (Colossians 3:18-22).

Notice how well-balanced this teaching is. There is an interrelationship in society as a whole and in the family. Obedience to God-ordained authority is the only way to enjoy peace and harmony.

The Christian Citizen

Parents should teach their children respect for law and order. The laws of our land may not be perfect, but without them we would only have chaos. Many chafe at any law at all, but what community could exist without rules and regulations governing the actions of its citizens? Here's one passage from the Bible dealing with this important matter:

"Submit yourselves to every ordinance of man for the Lord's sake: whether it be to the king, as supreme; or unto governors, as unto them that are sent by him for the punishment of evildoers, and for the praise of them that do well. For so is the will of God, that with well doing ye may put to silence the ignorance of foolish men: as free, and not using your liberty for a cloak of maliciousness, but as the servants of God. Honor all men. Love the brotherhood. Fear God. Honor the king" (1 Peter 2:13-17).

Whether we agree with every law on the books or not, we are not pleasing the Lord when we deliberately flout the civil statutes of our community and land.

Obedience covers the laws that seem insignificant as well as the more vital ones. What about speeding?

traffic signs? "No Dumping" and "No Hunting" signs? Do we have a right to obey only the ones we choose? What if everyone decided which ones to observe and which to ignore? Doesn't the golden rule apply here? Shouldn't we treat others the way we want to be treated? Do you want someone speeding down your street while your children are outside playing? Would you be pleased with someone who runs a stop sign and endangers your life?

Income tax time can be a test of character. Certainly it is right to take all the exemptions we are due. But to cheat on our tax return is stealing just as much as any other kind of theft. Some have refused to pay taxes because they felt the money wasn't spent right. Is this a matter for each individual to decide? Not if we are going to live by the Bible.

The principle has been established: as Christians we must obey the laws of the city, state, and nation in which we live. We must respect the officers of the land. This is right. And by doing it we will bring honor to our Lord. That's what we want, isn't it?

What About Church?

How often have you heard comments about the lack of reverence Protestants demonstrate toward the house of God? Such an attitude indicates lack of respect for the ministry and instruction of the church.

God gave much teaching along this line to the nation of Israel. The people were to hold their religious leaders in highest regard. God chose them and put them in their positions, so every worshiper was to give them respect.

The minister today occupies a sacred place before the congregation. He cannot forgive their sins, but he instructs them in the commandments and laws of God, which they should heed.

We should put into practice the instruction of Hebrews 13:7: "Remember them which have the rule over you, who have spoken unto you the word of God: whose faith follow, considering the end of their conversation."

If people do not respect the minister and obey him, in most instances they will not obey the Bible. Their appreciation of God is usually only as great as their love and devotion to their minister. The faithful, God-fearing minister respects this relationship and does nothing that would bring shame upon it.

Church organization is ordained of the Lord. It has the sanction of the New Testament. God has placed pastors, evangelists, and teachers in the church, as well as deacons and other leaders. Without such leadership the work of God could not go forward.

There is room for honest disagreement among Christians. No true leader claims to be infallible. His judgment is not always perfect. But this doesn't justify a spirit of rebellion against authority. People who rise up against the leadership of the church invariably hurt themselves spiritually. If the leader is wrong God will call him to account. Those who try to punish him themselves bring nothing but confusion and chaos to the situation.

Does Obedience Pay?

In Leviticus 26:3,4 God promised Israel: "If ye . . . keep my commandments, and do them; then I will give you rain in due season, and the land shall yield her increase, and the trees of the field shall yield their fruit." Thus, it was made clear to the people that obedience to God brought rewards.

Of course, we may see an individual who is ungodly and yet prosperous. However, this does not indicate by any means that disobedience and success automatically go together. The one who does not serve God may prosper temporarily. But in the end his path leads to sorrow, disappointment, and frustration. And remember, as Christians we are living not only for this world but also for the next.

The Scriptures even speak of long life as a reward for obedience. Listen to Proverbs 3:1,2: "My son, forget not my law; but let thine heart keep my commandments: for length of days, and long life, and peace, shall they add to thee."

Of course, we can point out instances where a Christian died young, but it is definitely true that obedience to the laws of God and man tends to enhance physical health and promote long life. How many there are whose lives are cut short by dissipation. Others meet an untimely death as a result of association with the wrong company. The evidence is definitely on the side of obedience. It promotes peace of mind and a clear conscience, which surely helps the nervous system and the rest of the body.

Last, but far from least, obedience assures us a home in heaven. Jesus said in Matthew 7:21: "Not every one that saith unto me, Lord, Lord, shall enter into the kingdom of heaven; but he that doeth the will of my Father which is in heaven."

ISAIAH 33: 15, 16

4 It's the Best Policy

"Honesty is the best policy." You've heard that often, haven't you? As far as a Christian is concerned, it's the *only* policy. Any deviation is unthinkable.

Here's God's yardstick: "Providing for honest things, not only in the sight of the Lord, but also in the sight of men" (2 Corinthians 8:21). We have to be concerned with both the eye of the Lord and the eye of man. God is watching us, and so are men. We can't afford to be halfhearted in our honesty.

What a beating honesty has been taking in our time! Many folks think you're stupid if you even *try* to be honest. Take the other fellow before he takes you—that's the philosophy of society today. But it's completely anti-Christian.

Occasions for dishonesty present themselves to us constantly. How easy it is to pretend to be asleep when someone calls us. Or to tell someone we forgot an appointment we didn't want to keep. Or to forget that item on our income tax. Or to pretend to be sick at church time on Sunday. We could go on and on.

When tax collectors asked John the Baptist, "What shall we do then?" his reply was very blunt: "Exact no more than that which is appointed you" (Luke 3:10,13). That was plain talk to men who were in the habit of charging excessively so they could get their "cut."

When soldiers asked John the Baptist what they should do, he replied, "Neither accuse any falsely" (v. 14). Those fellows lived by lying. The preacher's message probably wasn't very welcome.

In both these cases John the Baptist was laying heavy emphasis on honesty. He made it plain that men can't be right with God and crooked at the same time.

Honesty is something you have to work at. Paul said: "And herein do I exercise myself, to have always a conscience void of offense toward God, and toward men" (Acts 24:16). It takes some real "exercising" to live straight in times like these!

Here's another command from the Bible: "Provide things honest in the sight of all men" (Romans 12:17). No matter what that clever friend may say, this is what God says!

Didn't Jesus say it all when He gave us the golden rule: "And as ye would that men should do to you, do ye also to them likewise" (Luke 6:31)? You want *others* to be honest with *you*, don't you?

Be Honest With Yourself

The man who is not honest with himself will not be honest with others. What was the biggest accusation Jesus leveled against the Pharisees? Hypocrisy! They pretended to be what they weren't. They had convinced themselves they were all right. They were thoroughly dishonest with their own souls.

Hypocrite comes from a Greek word meaning "actor." Those men had put on an act until they believed it themselves. A skillful actor becomes very convincing. He actually seems to be the person he is portraying. Sad to say, not all actors are on the stage. You find them in just about every realm of life—folks who pretend to be what they aren't. They have done it so long they have convinced themselves they are true.

Sometimes this acting is done for money. Or, it may be to make a good social impression or influence someone politically. Some probably do it just to be well thought of. At any rate, it is a tragedy when anyone practices dishonesty with himself.

It's possible, of course, to trample our conscience underfoot until our hypocrisy doesn't bother us anymore. But this doesn't erase our guilt in God's sight. *He* is never fooled by our masks! We think we are playing our little part cleverly, but it doesn't impress the Lord. His eye sees right through every disguise. How often do you hear someone say, "Don't kid yourself"? But many are doing just that. As Christians let's be sure we aren't among them.

Through Isaiah God told us who is acceptable with Him: "He that walketh righteously, and speaketh uprightly; he that despiseth the gain of oppressions, that shaketh his hands from holding of bribes, that stoppeth his ears from hearing of blood, and shutteth his eyes from seeing evil; he shall dwell on high; his place of defense shall be the munitions of rocks: bread shall be given him; his waters shall be sure" (Isaiah 33:15,16). The conditions of this promise can be boiled down to one word—*honesty.*

Before there can be a policy of honesty there must be an honest person. Proverbs 16:7,8 says: "When a man's ways please the Lord, he maketh even his enemies to be at peace with him. Better is a little with righteousness, than great revenues without right." A man's ways aren't going to please the Lord if those ways are dishonest. The honest man with his little will have peace of conscience that forever eludes the grasp of others. He can sleep at night; he doesn't have to lie awake trying to remember what lies he has told during the day.

A Little Sand

A man said: "For years when I have bowed down in private prayer, a certain incident in my life has been slapping me in the face." The man was over 80, and wealthy. He had given thousands of dollars to missions and the cause of education. But a little sand within caused friction.

He continued: "Years ago I bought some hay from a neighbor. It was weighed and I gave the man the totals. Before the account was settled the man died. I went to the administrator and asked if he had any account against me. He found nothing, and I gave the claim no further attention. But the matter has put a shadow on my life for years. It has hindered my spiritual progress. Tomorrow morning I am going to the widow and settle the account in full." He did just that, and the inward battle was over. He had liberty again.

Honesty in Business

Deut 25:13-16

Among the greatest temptations is dishonesty in business dealings. Many yield for the purpose of making a "fast buck." Some contend that such things are simply part of making a living. But we must view it through God's eyes. He never condones such actions. He condemns them.

We could quote Scripture passages all day long regarding this matter. For the sake of brevity we'll hold it down. But how about this one:

"Thou shalt not have in thy bag divers weights, a great and a small: thou shalt not have in thine house divers measures, a great and a small: but thou shalt have a perfect and just weight, a perfect and just measure shalt thou have: that thy days may be lengthened in the land which the Lord thy God giveth thee. For all that do such things, and all that do unrighteously, are an abomination unto the Lord thy God" (Deuteronomy 25:13-16).

That passage doesn't need any explanation, does it? Here's another:

"He that hath not given forth upon usury, neither hath taken any increase, that hath withdrawn his hand from iniquity, hath executed true judgment between man and man, hath walked in my statutes, and hath kept my judgments, to deal truly; he is just, he shall surely live, saith the Lord God" (Ezekiel 18:8,9).

These two passages are from the Old Testament. With all the commandments God gave His people, He was greatly concerned about their honesty in business as well as their performance of the ritual of the Law. Has God changed? A thousand times, no.

Staying honest in business really keeps a Christian on his toes. He must be sure he doesn't make false claims for his products. Today's advertising certainly involves exaggeration. Should a Christian go along with this? Not if he wants to keep his testimony. As the passage from Deuteronomy emphasizes, God's child must make sure his weights and measures are accurate.

What should a Christian do if he gets the wrong change from the cashier—too much, that is? The answer is obvious.

The truth is twisted so often today that many do not know what honesty really is. A Christian has to keep close to the Bible to avoid being swept up in this current.

Do schools teach enough about honesty and integrity? Do churches emphasize character building as strongly as they should? Are we interested in building churches or in building lives?

The sad truth is a whole generation has grown up that knows little about real honesty. Efforts to defraud the public are commonplace. The rule of business seems to be, "What a person doesn't know won't hurt him." So if you can get an extra dollar from a customer you're justified in doing it, for he will never miss it.

What About Employees?

Most of our discussion has seemed to point to the employer—the boss. What about the worker? Honesty as an employee involves not only refusing to steal money, but also giving a full day's work for a full day's pay. It is dishonest to steal an employer's time as well as his cash.

What about drawing sick pay when you're not really sick? Or drawing unemployment pay when you could easily get a job?

A Tax Collector Meets Jesus

Zaccheus was a publican—a tax collector. The more he could gouge from people the more he could keep for himself. His bad reputation was known all over Jericho. Probably he had stifled his conscience to the point where he felt no guilt. "Other publicans do it," he may have told himself.

But when Zaccheus came under the influence of Jesus he became conscious of his sin. In fact, his guilt became so heavy that he cried out for forgiveness (Luke 19:1-10).

It's the same with us. If we keep away from Christian influence our eyes will become blinded to the wrongs of modern business practices. But if we are faithful to church, prayer, and Bible reading our spiritual and moral sensitivity will stay sharp.

A Christian in the used-car business will tell a potential customer the real condition of the car he is thinking of buying. If he also repairs cars he will not do unnecessary work so he can charge more.

The car business is not the only one that needs Christian principles. We simply cite it as an example. The practice of dishonesty has swept across our whole nation and infected every realm. God's people must resist this spirit as fiercely as they resist Communism or false religion. They must stay as far away from it as they would from disease germs.

Social Relationships

We must start right in the home to practice honesty. We must practice it with our parents, our children, and our brothers and sisters. Every relationship we have with one another should be aboveboard, honest, and upright. We owe each other a strict accounting of our actions toward each other. How easy it is to compliment to the face, and then criticize when' the back is turned. Dishonesty colors so many personal relationships. It produces disagreements, tension, and nervous disorders. No wonder divorce disrupts so many homes. When honesty does not exist between companions what else can you expect?

In our social contacts with friends and associates we have many temptations to stretch the truth. Sometimes there is strong pressure to deliberately lie to achieve some personal end. No one should have to be told that this displeases the Lord. But do we remember that it also weakens our Christian influence in our community? If God's people can't be trusted, who *can* be?

Should we borrow money from a friend when we know we can't pay it back? Should we make promises we know we can't keep? What about Christians in school: Is it worth the higher mark one might make on an exam if he has to cheat to gain it?

If we are honest in small things it will be easier to be honest in big things. It may seem trifling to fail to keep an appointment when we actually could have done so. The excuse we make to cover our negligence may seem insignificant. But every time we compromise it weakens our moral fabric. Small leaks become big ones. Eventually we may sink!

What an example we have in Joseph. He came to Egypt as a slave, but soon had a trusted position in the home of a high official. We read in Genesis 39:8,9 that Joseph said to his master's wife: "Behold, my master wotteth not what is with me in the house, and he hath committed all that he hath to my hand; there is none greater in this house than I; neither hath he kept back any thing from me but thee."

Potiphar was accustomed to slaves who were sneaky; who would steal at the slightest opportunity. He was unaccustomed to having employees who did not lie. There must have been something radiating from Joseph's life that made him know, "This man is different." The "something" was, of course, God's presence. He was a man deeply committed to the

Lord. Honesty was a natural by-product of his spiritual experience.

Dr. Will H. Houghton, the late president of Moody Bible Institute, told of a soldier who finally became a Christian through seeing his companions make fun of another soldier who was a believer in Christ. What impressed him was that, although they made fun of this man, they left their money in his possession for safekeeping.

The world gives no heed to the all-seeing Eye that watches every act of man. Christians must never let this truth escape them. There are many things we may get away with as far as other humans are concerned, but each act is recorded in a Book that will be opened on a coming day. This is not "scare talk." It is Biblical truth. Nothing can be concealed from the great Judge.

What About Outsiders?

Is our policy of honesty to apply only to fellow Christians? Of course not. Listen to Paul's words in 1 Thessalonians 4:11, 12: "And that ye study to be quiet, and to do your own business, and to work with your own hands, as we commanded you; that ye may walk honestly toward them that are without, and that ye may have lack of nothing." Obviously, "them that are without" are the unsaved; those outside the church.

One of the most important aspects of a Christian's life is his relationship to the unsaved. They aren't reading the Bible, but they are reading the life of God's child. Many who could not be won by a sermon are won by the consistent living of a Christian.

If there is a time when we need to be especially cautious concerning honesty it is when we are dealing with someone who is not a Christian. Such people are often looking for a weak spot in us. The slightest letdown in honesty will give them ammunition to shoot at us the rest of our lives. Worst of all, it may keep them from church and from salvation. There just isn't any room for a Christian to compromise when it comes to honesty.

5 Stay in Command!

When you're driving your car you have to keep hold of the steering wheel. You don't dare let go and trust the car to stay in the right lane of its own accord. You're in command. You're the driver. It's your responsibility to keep your vehicle under control.

This is true in life. The Bible teaches self-control. *You* are responsible for controlling *you*. There are plenty of forces trying to take the steering wheel out of your hands. It's up to you to say, "No," to all of them. You have to stay in command or you may wreck your life—and others, too.

"Every man that striveth for the mastery is temperate in all things." That's what Paul wrote in 1 Corinthians 9:25. The *New American Standard Bible* makes it clearer: "And everyone who competes in the games exercises self-control in all things."

Paul frequently used athletic illustrations and this is one of them. An athlete trying to win a race must exercise great self-discipline. He must say, "No," to himself when he feels a craving for heavy desserts, late hours, and extra sleep. He does it for a prize that is of little value. In fact, in Paul's day it was only a wreath placed on the victor's head. Paul's argument was that if such an insignificant prize was worth such self-discipline, how much more is the eternal prize for which the Christian strives.

There are passions and desires that are legitimate, but which will destroy the soul if they get out of hand. There are many things connected with the physical side of life that must be restrained for the sake of the spiritual.

Discipline is always somewhat distasteful, but like some other distasteful things it is a necessity. All the rewards for a life of self-control are not postponed until eternity. We will begin to receive benefits immediately.

We live in a day when old restraints, standards, and barriers are being swept away. Much is said about "self-expression." It is a time of great lawlessness. Many think they have no obligation to anything but their own will. In all too many cases, passions and desires are gratified regardless of the cost or results. No wonder a terrible wave of moral degeneracy is sweeping the nation and the world. Christians are not immune to such temptations. We must fight them vigorously. Self-control must be our way of life.

Start on the Inside

"He that hath no rule over his own spirit is like a city that is broken down, and without walls" (Proverbs 25:28).

The person who can't control himself will certainly be controlled by forces stronger than he. Unless he learns to master himself he will always be a slave to something.

A city like the one mentioned in the above verse is undefended. It is open to the first invader that comes along. The man who puts no restraint on his passions, desires, and affections is like such a city. He has no defense when temptations come. Having lost his self-control he is certain to be carried away by the forces of sin.

We'd better look into our own hearts and check our self-control. Not only does this affect us, but every person with whom we associate. An example is pointed out in Proverbs 15:18: "A wrathful man stirreth up strife: but he that is slow to anger appeaseth strife." The man who cannot control his wrath causes trouble for everyone. Without warning he may give vent to violent language, or he may go even further and become physically abusive.

Speaking of anger, there is probably no area of life that is a greater testing ground for self-control. The man who can control and restrain his anger will develop a strong character. He will have great influence for righteousness.

Outbursts of temper often put scars on the hearts of loved ones. When we feel an urge to express our anger we should immediately take ourselves in hand and, with God's help, exercise discipline over our spirit. After the storm of temper has passed and we have quieted down we will be happy if we have mastered the impulse to say something harsh. And it will be much easier to win the victory the next time.

There are other passions besides temper. Our basic passions could probably be classified as love, hate, anger, fear, joy, ardor, and jealousy. These may, of course, assert themselves in good ways as well as evil. But we must be sure we are in command of them and can direct them into the right channels.

We must also be able to control our desires. Here again, desires may be both good and bad. Many things are legitimate until they are carried to the extreme. That is where self-control comes in. This would include even ambition, which is good and necessary unless it gets the upper hand and enslaves us.

Check These Scripture Passages

We won't take the space to quote these Scripture passages, but for your own benefit you should look them up. They advocate control of the various passions that are part of our lives:

Anger—Proverbs 14:17,29. Hate—Proverbs 15:17; 1 John 2:9; 4:20. Fear—Deuteronomy 6:2; Joshua 1:9; Proverbs 1:7; Matthew 10:28. Love—Song of Solomon 8:6,7; Mark 12:30,31; John 13:34,35; 1 John 4:18,20. Jealousy—1 Samuel 18:8,9; Proverbs 6:34,35. Joy—Exodus 15:2; Deuteronomy 26:11; 2 Corinthians 1:24. Ardor—Judges 7:5-7; 2 Samuel 6:16; Matthew 13:20, 21; Mark 10:17-22.

Desires

Desires can be good or bad. It is entirely up to us which way they go. This is where self-control comes in. Moderation must be learned and achieved.

What about ambition? It's good and necessary. A person without it isn't worth much. But there are times when men can become too ambitious. The disciples had this problem. They all wanted to be the greatest. Each one had dreams of having the highest place in Christ's kingdom. Jesus had to warn them that the real way to climb high was to start out low. He said that desiring to be "first" was a sure way to end up last (Mark 9:33-37).

Have you heard of Haman, the man who was hanged on his own scaffold? He's a character in the Book of Esther. He was so anxious to climb to the top that he planned the death of his chief rival, Mordecai, a Jew. But in the end Mordecai was promoted and Haman was hanged. That may be an extreme example, but there have been some sad stories of lives where ambition got out of control.

Even spiritual ambition can be a problem. Remember Simon, the sorcerer of Samaria? When he saw believers filled with the Spirit through the laying on of the apostles' hands, he wanted the same power. In fact, he even offered to buy it! Naturally it isn't for sale, and Peter put him in his place in a hurry. Simon saw an opportunity to occupy a high place in the church. Imagine having people flock to him to have his hands laid on them! He got the props knocked out from under him very fast (Acts 8:9-24).

Then there is that ugly word *covetousness*. Why is it that something another person owns always seems better than what we have? To wish for something like that which others possess is not entirely wrong. It's a natural trait. But natural traits can get the best of us if we don't keep the upper hand. If you find yourself wanting something so badly that you are willing to do anything to get it, watch out! Coveting can lead to a complete sacrifice of principles. It sometimes affects morals and can lead to restraint's being thrown to the four winds.

Somewhere along the line we have to make a decision about how far our desires are going to go. We must not permit ourselves to covet. To do so is sin. Continuing in it will bring God's judgment.

"The wicked boasteth of his heart's desire, and blesseth the covetous, whom the Lord abhorreth." Those are strong words. It shocks some people to hear about God's "abhorring." But those words are found in Psalm 10:3. They are God's warning to us.

Listen to Jesus: "Take heed, and beware of covetousness: for a man's life consisteth not in the abundance of the things which he possesseth" (Luke 12:15).

Paul's attitude toward covetousness is the right one: "I have coveted no man's silver, or gold, or apparel" (Acts 20:33). What was his secret? It was this: "I have learned, in whatsoever state I am, therewith to be content" (Philippians 4:11).

Thoughts

Isn't everyone an expression of the thoughts that are in his heart? Proverbs 23:7 says: "For as he thinketh in his heart, so is he."

Remember how wicked man was before the Flood? Do you know what God said about men's thinking in those days? Here it is: "And God saw that the wickedness of man was great in the earth, and that every imagination of the thoughts of his heart was only evil continually" (Genesis 6:5). The Lord knew that men's wickedness started in their thoughts.

There is a tremendous battle in progress today. It isn't being waged with guns. It's the battle for the human mind. God wants the mind, and so does Satan. Think how many forces are aimed at men's thoughts today. Radio, television, magazines, newspapers, and books all exert influence on man's thought life. It takes real self-control to withstand the subtle power of these means of communication. But we can, and we must.

The Chinese have a proverb: "He who can govern himself is fit to govern the world." But no one can govern himself unless he starts inside his head. He must take charge of his thoughts and keep them under the strictest control. If he doesn't, they will destroy him.

"Outer" Control

We've been talking about self-control on the inside of us. What about the outside? We're physical as well as spiritual. We have bodies as well as minds. Control in this area is also vital.

Our body is a gift of God. Usually it functions well if it is treated right. But God has designed laws for the regulation of the body, and if we break them we'll pay the penalty.

Strange as it may seem, the Bible has a good deal to say about gluttony. That's abusing the body by overeating. Here's one passage: "When thou sittest to eat with a ruler, consider diligently what is before thee: and put a knife to thy throat, if thou be a man given to appetite" (Proverbs 23:1,2). Anything that harms us physically is displeasing to God. It is a medical fact that many people are literally eating themselves to death. Self-control might lengthen life!

We've heard a lot in recent years about the harm done by tobacco. In addition to the physical harm, it is an enslaving habit that a Christian should have no part of.

Is it necessary to devote much space to the harm done by alcohol? It attacks its victims physically, mentally, spiritually, and morally. Not one good thing can be said about the use of such poison. There is only one stand for a Christian to take regarding alcohol in any form. It is total abstinence. Besides the personal harm he would suffer, think of his example to others. Wouldn't you hate to be the cause of someone's becoming an alcoholic?

Here are some more Scripture verses to check: Proverbs 25:16; Romans 13:14; 1 Corinthians 9:27.

And oh, that tongue! Talk about needing control—nothing needs it more! It can do lots of good and also lots of damage. We are the ones who decide which. A few wrong words can bring heartbreak and even ruin someone's character. Churches have been divided and weakened when some member failed to control his or her tongue. Malicious slander and gossip have injured the reputations of too many. Let's always be sure our words are helpful and not harmful.

Anyone can tear down with his talk. It takes intelligence and consecration to build up people. Words of encouragment are sorely needed. A few words by a Christian worker changed the direction of D. L. Moody's life. Control your tongue, and your life will be blessed and will bless others. James 3:2 says: "If any man offend not in word, the same is a perfect man, and able also to bridle the whole body." (Also read verses 4-18).

Can It Really Be Done?

Is self-control actually possible? Or is it an impossible dream? Let's answer by saying it is entirely possible if one really *wants* to. If someone does not care whether he controls himself or not, he will never do it. When we determine to follow God's will and purpose we'll reach our goal. There may be some failures along the way, but we'll use them as steppingstones and go right on.

We are told in Daniel 1:8 that "Daniel purposed in his heart that he would not defile himself with the portion of the king's meat, nor with the wine which he drank." Daniel won his battle. The victory began when he purposed in his heart to remain true to God. Tremendous pressure was put on him, but he resisted and refused to compromise his convictions.

In 1 Corinthians 9:27 Paul said: "But I keep under my body, and bring it into subjection." If we don't rule our body, it will rule us. Be sure you rule your physical impulses instead of letting them rule you. Try denying yourself occasionally, even though it may be something legitimate you desire. The discipline of saying "no" to your own desires will strengthen your self-control and self-mastery.

Whenever possible, steer clear of tempting situations. Don't stick your head in the lion's mouth and then ask God not to let him bite it off! Don't intentionally walk into something that threatens to rob your self-control. Choose your company carefully. Associate with those who help, rather than hinder you spiritually and morally.

Above all, remember that God stands ready to help you at all times. It is His will that you be an overcomer. Never fail to call on Him in the hour of trial. Don't wait until the emergency arises. Make prayer a daily habit. Such a practice will strengthen you for the test when it comes. Make a constant companion of your Bible. Its promises, warnings, and teachings will put steel in your character.

If you sometimes fail, don't let discouragement drive you into permanent defeat. God's hand will be stretched out to help you get up again. Refuse to allow tormenting thoughts of past defeats to get you down. Say with Paul: "I can do all things through Christ which strengtheneth me" (Philippians 4:13).

Rewards A-plenty

You don't have to wait for heaven to reap all of your reward for practicing self-control. There are multitudes of blessings even in this present life. A strong body, a good conscience, a clear mind, good relations with others, a happy home—all these benefits go along with self-control. And at the end of the road is the city of God.

This life is not the end. There is another, better life to come. Those who are slaves to themselves are living only for the present and ignoring eternity. The ultimate end for those who are ruled by their appetites is described in Philippians 3:19: "Whose end is destruction, whose God is their belly, and whose glory is in their shame, who mind earthly things." (Also read Proverbs 21:17; 1 Timothy 5:6; and 2 Peter 2:13.)

All fleshly appetites *can* be controlled. In some instances there will be total abstinence; in others, moderation and temperance. The great prize for which the Christian is striving is worth all the discipline required. The reward here is great; the reward hereafter is beyond comprehension.

Keep the steering wheel of life in your hands, Christian. Don't let anything jerk it out of your grasp. Be the master—not the mastered. Never forget that in your great goal of self-control you always have God on your side!

6 Keep Your Cool

The last chapter was about self-control. This one concerns *patience*. They're pretty closely related. The Bible has plenty to say about both.

The dictionary has some interesting definitions of *patience*. The word *patient* comes from a Latin word meaning "to suffer." Sometimes this is exactly what patience is!

"The quality of suffering without complaint; endurance and perseverance; forbearance; the power to wait calmly." These are some of the expressions the dictionary uses to define patience. Some synonyms for *patience* are composure, fortitude, resignation, and submission.

It's easy to feel that patience is something a person has to be born with. If we don't have it there's nothing we can do about it. That's how we often reason. It isn't true, though. Patience is a quality of character that usually does not come to us automatically. It must be developed. Naturally we develop it only through tests. We must face experiences in which our patience is tried. The trial can be pretty fierce, too.

Patience involves enduring situations without complaint. Sometimes this even means suffering. Patience is the ability to stay unruffled. It is an inner quality, although it expresses itself outwardly. It has its roots deep within the soul. Let's never forget that if we lack patience God can help us develop it. He won't drop it into our life in one big bundle, but He'll help us master the lessons that will produce patience.

Many difficult experiences occur in our lives. Often we want to break free from them. The tests may last so long that we wonder, "Will this ever stop?" We try to find answers and often fail.

What we must keep in mind is that our difficulties are not unique. Somewhere in the world there are others who have fought the same battles we fight. There are people just like us who have endured situations like ours and learned patience through them. Our problems do have answers. What we have to develop is the willingness to be calm if those answers don't come right away. We're in a hurry, but God works slowly. Weeds grow fast, but not character. And God is willing to take time. The greatest example of all is Jesus. Keep your eyes on Him and not on your own shortcomings.

When Things Are Tough

"Rejoicing in hope; patient in tribulation." That's what Paul wrote in Romans 12:12. It's a high goal, but we should never stop aiming at it.

This world is full of suffering, sorrow, injustice, and trouble. It's natural to ask, "Why?" Often the "why" must be left with God. People who don't know the Lord become terribly angry about these things. Sometimes they lash out violently against them. This is not the way for the Christian to handle difficult situations.

Let's shun the deadly plague of self-pity. We are prone to think our lot is worse than anyone else's. If we convince ourselves of this, despair easily takes hold. This is exactly what Satan wants. Discouragement is his best weapon.

We must keep reminding ourselves, "With God's help I can get the best of this." And you can! It's no dream; it's scriptural. "I can do all things through Christ which strengtheneth me," Paul declared in Philippians 4:13. He wasn't about to throw in the towel, even though he was writing from a prison.

Being patient is not a matter of gritting your teeth, clenching your fists, and muttering, "I hate this, but I guess I have to take it!" It's a matter of committing things to the Lord and letting His peace take over in your heart.

James wrote in James 5:11: "Ye have heard of the patience of Job." Probably no Biblical character is so well-known for patience. He lost his property, his servants, his children, and finally his health. Yet he continually expressed his faith in God. When his children were killed he bowed himself and worshiped God instead of complaining. His only word was: "The Lord gave, and the Lord hath taken away; blessed be the name of the Lord" (Job 1:21). The Bible says further: "In all this Job sinned not, nor charged God foolishly" (v. 22).

Suffering? Job had plenty of it. On top of all his burdens his supposed friends criticized him severely. They even declared that the trouble he was having was the result of his sins. It wasn't true, of course. Job's own wife advised him to curse God and die. Fortunately he didn't follow her suggestion; he kept his faith and his godly character. And he was rewarded, for we read in Job 42:12: "So the Lord blessed the latter end of Job more than his beginning."

Never forget that God himself puts a limit on our trials. He has never given anyone more than he can bear. And He never will. He has promised.

What About Folks Who "Bug" You?

One of the greatest tests of patience is in our relationships with other human beings. Everyone has likes and dislikes, peculiarities, ambitions, and convictions. When all of these jostle against the same characteristics in others, there may be a clash.

Paul wrote: "Now we exhort you, brethren . . . be patient toward all men" (1 Thessalonians 5:14). That's a big "all." But the Bible is the only safe rule to use. If left to ourselves we would be patient toward some and explode at others.

All of our enduring does not involve persecution and mistreatment. We must also learn patience with people who are ill-tempered, strong-willed, and selfish. They may have other characteristics that clash with our own personalities. Sometimes such people work on the same job as we. They may be in the same class in school. They might even be in the same home or the same church. No matter where you turn, there is an opportunity to exercise the great virtue of patience.

Remember Jesus' experience. Have you stopped to think what He had to endure in His associations with others? He knew from the beginning that one of His apostles, Judas, had a traitor's heart. Even before the betrayal Judas showed an ugly spirit many times. Peter was unstable. He was always speaking out of turn. James and John wanted to call down fire from heaven on the Samaritans because of their lack of hospitality. It must have been with a little smile that

Jesus nicknamed them "the sons of thunder." But their hot tempers were no joke.

The disciples quarreled about who should be the greatest. The sons of Zebedee got their mother to intercede with Jesus. She asked that her boys be given the highest places of honor in His kingdom (Matthew 20:20-28). Childish? Selfish? Irritating? Of course!

Even Jesus' mother didn't always understand Him. His own brothers and sisters didn't believe in Him. Some of His relatives thought He was crazy. But He dealt with all of these people with such kindness, gentleness, and patience that we can only marvel as we read the story.

Why do workers in the office try to irritate you? Why do so many people at church ignore you? Why does that neighbor always burn his trash when your clothes have just been hung out on the line? Can't he stop his dog from barking in the middle of the night?

There are a multitude of things that cause friction between people. But they need not. Patience can smooth out every situation.

Paul Had His Problems

Paul, the greatest of the apostles, had trials in his relations with other people. He and Barnabas had a sharp disagreement over the latter's nephew, Mark. The young man went on a missionary journey with them, only to become homesick and turn back. Through the years of walking with Christ, Paul learned the secret of patience. In 2 Timothy 4:11 he wrote: "Take Mark, and bring him with thee: for he is profitable to me for the ministry."

So you're not the only one who has had to learn through experience. Even Paul had to struggle with an impatient nature. He was a stern disciplinarian, and his sternness turned to impatience at times.

Just for preaching the gospel, Paul was led into many hard situations. He was mistreated, imprisoned, beaten, left for dead, misunderstood, and lied about. Yet he did not retaliate. Patiently he continued to urge men to accept Christ even when they snarled at him like wild beasts.

Only after practicing great patience could Paul write to the Colossians: "That ye might walk worthy of the Lord unto all pleasing, being fruitful in every good work, and increasing in the knowledge of God; strengthened with all might, according to his glorious power, unto all patience and long-suffering with joyfulness" (1:10,11).

Later in this Epistle Paul wrote: "Put on therefore, as the elect of God, holy and beloved, bowels of mercies, kindness, humbleness of mind, meekness, longsuffering; forbearing one another, and forgiving one another, if any man have a quarrel against any: even as Christ forgave you, so also do ye" (3:12).

To the Ephesians the apostle wrote: "I therefore, the prisoner of the Lord, beseech you that ye walk worthy of the vocation wherewith ye are called, with all lowliness and meekness, with long-suffering, forbearing one another in love" (4:1,2).

Paul knew that many were looking to him as an example. How faithfully he established the pattern of patience for us! To confirm this he wrote in 2 Corinthians 6:4-6: "But in all things approving ourselves as the ministers of God, in much *patience*, in afflictions, in necessities, in distresses, in stripes, in imprisonments, in tumults, in labors, in watchings, in fastings; by pureness, by knowledge, by *long-suffering*, by kindness. . . ."

Paul gave importance to patience by granting it equal place with signs, wonders, and mighty deeds in the minister's and the believer's life. In 2 Corinthians 12:12 he wrote: "Truly the signs of an apostle were wrought among you in all *patience,* in signs, and wonders, and mighty deeds."

Your Testimony Is at Stake

To Timothy, Paul wrote: "The servant of the Lord must not strive; but be gentle unto all men, apt to teach, patient" (2 Timothy 2:24). As long as we are gentle and patient with all men there will be little chance of strife. It takes two to make a quarrel.

Where and to whom can we show patience? "Toward all men" was Paul's rule. We can exhibit patience under every circumstance of life and to every person. To our friends, relatives, business associates, business competitors, political opponents, and athletic opponents we must show patience. Paul called God "the God of patience and consolation." He thus acknowledged that help in being patient comes from the Lord. Then he added the prayer that God would "grant you to be likeminded one toward another according to Christ Jesus" (Romans 15:5).

Most of Paul's lessons came from suffering. We may not be physically mistreated as he was, but the chances are that the lessons that teach us patience will be tough.

It Takes Some "Following After"

"But thou, O man of God . . . follow after . . . patience. . . ." That's what Paul wrote to Timothy in 1 Timothy 6:11.

Patience is a thing to be sought after. It is to be pursued. No one can acquire it overnight. It must be developed over a period of time. This happens as we meet various experiences and learn to handle them with calm trust in God.

Knowing that we need patience and securing it are not the same thing. As a starting point we need to know the ideal toward which we are striving. Then every effort can be exerted to learn patience.

No halfhearted individual can expect to develop patience. Second Peter 1:5,6 says: "And besides this, giving all diligence, add to your faith virtue; and to virtue, knowledge; and to knowledge, temperance; and to temperance, *patience;* and to patience, godliness."

Each step of progress in Christian living makes the next step possible. Failure at any point reduces the chance of success. But it does not mean definite failure. We can still retrace our steps, find out where we stumbled, and try again. Since human nature is subject to failures, this is the course most of us will take. Be determined; never give up. Keep your goal in mind. Know that it *can be attained.*

That passage from 2 Peter (1:5,6) shows that the Christian life is an experience of constantly adding on. One virtue is added to another. Notice that patience is listed between temperance (self-control) and godliness. This indicates that it's the link between the two. There is a close relationship between patience and godliness.

Hebrews 12:1 takes us to the athletic field: "Let us run with patience the race that is set before us." Running the race patiently takes practice—lots of it. No runner can carefully calculate his pace or distance without practice. He must run the course many times to learn patience in controlling his speed and strength for the final spurt. We must practice patience to possess it. Over and over again we must remind ourselves of what we must do, and then, with God's help, do it.

Maybe it sounds strange to associate running with patience. Unconsciously we think patience is passive. We could more easily think of someone being patient while he is lying down. Not so. The real test of patience comes during activity. If we could withdraw from the scene and rest, patience would come more easily. But to keep running and still exercise patience is the real test.

It's Worth All the Effort

Each adversity, injury, provocation, persecution, and abuse is an opportunity to display patience. The challenge to run with patience is an individual one. In a race each runner is on his own. In some respects Christian living is a very individual matter. There are many ways we can get help from others, but there are also times when we're on our own—but never without God.

The Bible itself is a tremendous help in our efforts to become more patient. Every verse we read about patience is a help in attaining our goal. Above all, don't become discouraged if you don't find yourself growing by leaps and bounds in the realm of patience. Progress may be slow at times, but keep everlastingly at it!

7 It Helps Lighten the Load

When you think of Jesus, what comes to your mind first? Probably it is His kindness. He did more than tolerate people. He constantly looked for ways to help them. Nothing lifts the load from a human heart like kindness. It doesn't have to be something big. Just a small act of kindness may work wonders.

Kindness and *kin* are closely related. In fact, *kindness* comes from the family word meaning "kin." To be kind to someone means to treat him as your "kin."

Kindness is more than just a series of good deeds performed coldly and mechanically. A warm inner nature motivates true kindness. Kind deeds spring from a kind heart. You can't fake kindness for long.

Everyone needs help in some way. We don't have to search long for ways to be kind. There's more to it than just keeping peace with others. A truly kind person actively looks for ways to help and be gracious.

It's easy to become preoccupied with our own little world. Our problems seem so big that we forget about those of others. We're always glad to *receive* help. Are we just as quick to *give* it?

Unfortunately there are folks who see a need, but have a clever way of avoiding responsibility for it.

They piously call someone *else's* attention to it, and then forget it.

Kindness is a personal responsibility. Usually it is a one-on-one proposition. There may be occasions when we help several people at a time, but most often it's just one. It's that personal touch that really lightens the load.

Is it necessary to wait until someone does *you* a favor before you show them kindness? Indeed not. This would make it simply an exchange. Jesus told us to do good to folks who can't repay us. That's the real Christian spirit.

Sometimes there is such a thing as negative kindness. This involves keeping quiet when we know something unfavorable about an individual. Some people get a thrill out of broadcasting such things. Christians shouldn't.

As always, Jesus is our foremost Example. We are told that He "went about doing good" (Acts 10:38). It is also written that He said: "It is more blessed to give than to receive" (20:35). On one occasion He declared: "For even the Son of man came not to be ministered unto, but to minister" (Mark 10:45).

It Means Just Plain "Doing Good"

Here's an Old Testament passage that shows God was trying to teach the law of kindness to His people long ago:

"Thou shalt not see thy brother's ox or his sheep go astray and hide thyself from them: thou shalt in any case bring them again unto thy brother. And if thy brother be not nigh unto thee, or if thou know him not, then thou shalt bring it unto thine own house, and it shall be with thee until thy brother seek after it, and thou shalt restore it to him again. In like manner shalt thou do with his ass; and so shalt thou do with his raiment; and with all lost things of thy brother's, which he hath lost, and thou hast found, shalt thou do likewise: thou mayest not hide thyself. Thou shalt not see thy brother's ass or his ox fall down by the way, and hide thyself from them: thou shalt surely help him to lift them up again" (Deuteronomy 22:1-4).

Did you think the Old Testament was full of harshness and coldness? Here's an example of kindness to people in everyday happenings like losing an animal or an article of clothing. Human nature would say, "Finders, keepers." God said, "Find the owner. Get it back to him." If the beast's owner was unknown the finder was to keep it until he was located.

Today we probably won't see someone struggling to lift up a fallen animal as this passage describes, but we may have a chance to help fix a flat tire or get a car out of a ditch. It may not be a piece of clothing that is lost; it's more apt to be a lost billfold. The look of gratitude on the face of the owner when you return it will be all the reward you need. Little things? Not really. They can be pretty big. And such acts of helpfulness are part of the development of our Christian character.

Here the golden rule pops up again. The whole core of the matter is simply treating the other fellow the way we want to be treated. We like to be helped, so let's help others. We appreciate having lost items returned, so let's return what *we* find.

We can't limit our kindness to those in our own circle of family and friends. Often we meet strangers who need help. It's terrible to be stranded in a strange community. Have you ever been helped by a total stranger? Did someone you never saw before stop by the side of the road to help you when you had car trouble?

There's a Biblical example of helping strangers in Genesis 24:17-20:

"And the servant ran to meet her, and said, Let me, I pray thee, drink a little water out of thy pitcher. And she said, Drink, my lord: and she hasted, and let down her pitcher upon her hand, and gave him drink. And when she had done giving him drink, she said, I will draw water for thy camels also, until they have done drinking. And she hasted, and emptied her pitcher into the trough, and ran again unto the well to draw water, and drew for all his camels."

This act of kindness was the factor in the choice of Rebekah as Isaac's bride.

Others Aren't So Fortunate

God forbid that we should turn a cold shoulder to the one who is poverty-stricken and wears shabby clothes. Even in this land of luxury there are many who barely have the necessities of life. Some are in dire circumstances because their health has failed.

Jesus promised in Matthew 10:42: "And whosoever shall give to drink unto one of these little ones a cup of cold water only in the name of a disciple, verily I say unto you, he shall in no wise lose his reward." This suggests that doing a small act of kindness for the most insignificant person will qualify you for a reward from the hand of the Lord. Of course, your motive in giving the cold water should be a desire to help, rather than merely the hope of a reward.

Helping the unfortunate does something for our own spirit. Selfishness makes us turn all our concern inward. When we turn our heart outward toward another it helps combat the spirit of selfishness. It mellows us. And there is something about being kind to one who has been ill-treated by life that makes you want to do it again. It is far more satisfying than heaping all your attention on yourself.

One Good Turn Deserves Another

Who likes a person who takes all the favors he can get but never gives any? Some acts of kindness stem from plain gratitude. It was that way in David's case, as we read in 2 Samuel 9:7:

"David said unto him, Fear not: for I will surely show thee kindness for Jonathan thy father's sake, and will restore thee all the land of Saul thy father; and thou shalt eat bread at my table continually."

While Saul had tried to take David's life, his son, Jonathan, proved to be a close friend of David. Jonathan recognized that David was God's choice as king. Rather than fighting it, he willingly went along with the Lord's will. Now that David was king and Jonathan had been killed in battle, David sought some way to show kindness to Jonathan's children. Finally he located Mephibosheth. He was a cripple and in need of help. David welcomed the chance to repay some of Jonathan's kindness, even though Jonathan was now dead.

First, David restored all of Saul's land to Mephibosheth. Then, he had him eat at David's table every day. Ordinarily all the heirs of the deposed king were either killed or banished. This was a great concession on David's part to have Saul's heir at his table. It was his way of expressing his gratitude for Jonathan's kindness to him.

So many acts of kindness have been done for us. We should recognize them and repay them with acts of kindness whenever we find an opportunity.

How would David have felt if he had exacted revenge on Saul's family instead of showing kindness? There might have been momentary satisfaction, but it would have caused a festering sore in his spirit. Kindness always leaves its beneficial influence long after the helpful act has been done. Kind people are easy to get along with. They don't harbor bitterness. They aren't sour. They are good neighbors and good friends. Most of all they are good Christians. They are a real testimony for the gospel.

Listen to the promise of Ephesians 6:7,8: "With good will doing service, as to the Lord, and not to men: knowing that whatsoever good thing any man doeth, the same shall he receive of the Lord, whether he be bond or free."

What we sow, we reap. This works in a good way as it does concerning evil. If we sow seeds of kindness we will reap them. When we are kind to others we will be repaid in kind. It's the only way to live.

No One Stands Alone

Paul wrote in Romans 15:1: "We then that are strong ought to bear the infirmities of the weak, and not to please ourselves." As Christians we have an obligation to our fellowman. No one can stand completely alone. We all need each other. God has ordained that we should be interdependent. Some are not as strong as others. So God says to the stronger, "You help the weak ones."

Some are stronger spiritually than others. Some have a greater mental capacity than others. There are those that have many talents, while others have few. Instead of becoming egotistical over our abilities, let's be kind to those who seem shortchanged.

We must do all we can to make their burden lighter. It's heavy enough without our adding scorn or criticism to it. You won't have any trouble finding the weak ones who need help. They're all around.

In Romans 15 Paul goes on to say: "Let every one of us please his neighbor for his good to edification. For even Christ pleased not himself; but, as it is written, The reproaches of them that reproached thee fell on me. For whatsoever things were written aforetime were written for our learning, that we through patience and comfort of the Scriptures might have hope. Now the God of patience and consolation grant you to be likeminded one toward another according to Christ Jesus: that ye may with one mind and one mouth glorify God, even the Father of our Lord Jesus Christ" (vv. 2-6).

What are some of the needs that the strong should help bear? In Galatians 6:1,2 Paul points out: "Brethren, if a man be overtaken in a fault, ye which are spiritual, restore such a one in the spirit of meekness; considering thyself, lest thou also be tempted. Bear ye one another's burdens, and so fulfill the law of Christ."

Some fall prey to temptation more easily than others. Criticism doesn't help. In fact, it drives the person lower. If we are mature spiritually we should try to help these people develop strength and stability. There may be an unseen strength in the other fellow's life. If we discover it our thinking toward him may change. He may not be as weak as he seems. Perhaps he could be a real overcomer with a little help.

And let's never forget that we may need help ourselves sometime. Right now it may not seem we could ever fall. But if it does happen we will want mercy extended to us, won't we? We'll appreciate kindness and not censure. So let's do unto others as we want them to do unto us!

Don't Try to Pass the Buck

We may try to evade our duty sometimes by shrugging our shoulders and saying, "There's really nothing I can do to help." But never forget that many times just a kind word is the finest thing that can be given. And it doesn't cost us a cent!

Eliphaz said to Job: "Thy words have upholden him that was falling, and thou hast strengthened the feeble knees" (Job 4:4). The Moffatt translation makes this testimony even more inspiring: "Your words have kept men on their feet." Only eternity will reveal how many might have lost out completely in the Christian life if it had not been for some kind words that kept them on their feet.

Someone has said: "Treat everybody with kindness, for everybody is having a hard time." We don't have to look far to find someone with a burden too heavy for him to carry alone. It may be a friend in church, in school, or elsewhere. We may be the key to his victory or defeat.

The full force of the issue of kindness is expressed in Ephesians 4:31,32. You will note it is both negative and positive: "Let all bitterness, and wrath, and anger, and clamor, and evil speaking, be put away from you, with all malice: and be ye kind one to another, tenderhearted, forgiving one another, even as God for Christ's sake hath forgiven you."

If you refrain from expressing bitterness, wrath, anger, evil speaking, and malice you will go a long way toward being kind to others. Many of the burdens people bear come because someone has abused them in some way. Often it has been through a tongue-lashing. To further the treatment for good Paul said: "Be ye kind one to another, tenderhearted, forgiving." It would be a great relief and a joy to be treated in such a way by everyone, wouldn't it? But even if it only happens occasionally it's refreshing. Let's make up our minds to be refreshers!

The kindness of a minister probably did more good than many of his sermons. A telephone operator was talking about him to her fellow worker: 'He's a patient man. I was flustered and gave him the wrong number four times, and he said so kindly, 'You know, operator, you gave me the wrong number four times. Try once again.' I'd like to meet that man." The other operator then inquired, "What is his number?" When she was told she said, "I know him. He is my pastor." "Then," replied the other, "I'm going to hear him preach."

Be a Sharer

Jesus predicted that when He comes to judge humanity He will say to one group: "For I was ahungered, and ye gave me meat: I was thirsty, and ye gave me drink: I was a stranger, and ye took me in: naked, and ye clothed me: I was sick, and ye visited me: I was in prison, and ye came unto me. Then shall the righteous answer him, saying, Lord, when saw we thee ahungered, and fed thee? or thirsty, and gave thee drink? When saw we thee a stranger, and took thee in? or naked, and clothed thee? Or when saw we thee sick, or in prison, and came unto thee? And the King shall answer and say unto them, Verily I say unto you, Inasmuch as ye have done it unto one of the least of these my brethren, ye have done it unto me" (Matthew 25:35-40).

At a glance you may see many of your acquaintances who fit into one or more of these categories. It is easy to neglect them and hope that someone else will help them. But the spirit of Christ is to help them yourself.

If we enjoy life's blessings it is Christian to share them with others. Abraham Lincoln said: "Die when I may, I want it to be said of me by those who knew me best that I always plucked a thistle and planted a flower where I thought a flower would grow." Goethe said: "Kindness is the golden chain by which society is bound together." King David declared in Psalm 41:1: "Blessed is he that considereth the poor: the Lord will deliver him in time of trouble."

The Scriptures promise in Isaiah 58:10: "And if thou draw out thy soul to the hungry, and satisfy the afflicted soul; then shall thy light rise in obscurity, and thy darkness be as the noonday." God has made it clear in His Word that He will reward the one who shows kindness to those in need.

Every need may not be physical or financial. It may be spiritual or emotional. There is nothing worse than feeling you are forgotten. Let's be sure no one we could help ever feels that way.

8 There's Nothing Wrong With Humble Pie

Humility is simply having the right estimate of yourself. It isn't necessary to grovel to be humble. You don't have to constantly speak lightly of your abilities. There is such a thing as false humility. It's easily detected, and there's nothing beautiful about it.

To recognize the talents God has given us is no disgrace. What's important is that we don't forget they are divine gifts. They aren't something over which we can get bigheaded.

The truly humble person is usually not conscious of it. No doubt you have heard the joke about the man who wrote a book *My Humility, and How I Attained It!* Humility shows itself in the way we act. In fact, it shows up in our general attitude. The individual who is always calling attention to his "humility" is probably very short of it.

To get off to a good start, let's inject two important Scripture verses about humility:

"With all lowliness and meekness, with long-suffering, forbearing one another in love" (Ephesians 4:2).

"Humble yourselves in the sight of the Lord, and he shall lift you up" (James 4:10).

Teachableness

Humility shows itself in willingness to be taught. Psalm 25:9 says: "The meek will he guide in judgment: and the meek will he teach his way." Here meekness and humility are synonymous. The one who is arrogant and proud feels no need to be taught. Not so with the humble person. He recognizes his need of learning something new every day. He submits gladly to God's authority. He bows without hesitation to the authority of the Scriptures. He knows that the fear of the Lord is the beginning of wisdom.

It is tragic that today so many have become disdainful of their elders. The humble individual realizes his elders have much to teach him. There is no one from whom we cannot learn something!

Know-it-alls are to be pitied. There are always a few of them around—quick to give advice but slow to take it. Refusal to accept counsel can be disastrous. We need instruction and guidance. It's no disgrace to seek help from others. Listen to Proverbs 12:15: "The way of a fool is right in his own eyes: but he that hearkeneth unto counsel is wise."

Self-sacrifice

Humility involves a willingness to give up personal ambition for public good. In this Moses was an outstanding example. He could have risen high in the ruling circles of Egypt. Instead he chose to lead the despised Israelites out of bondage.

Proverbs 16:19 says: "Better it is to be of a humble spirit with the lowly, than to divide the spoil with the proud." Moses practiced this. As the son of Pharaoh's daughter he "had it made." Yet he humbly sought his place among the lowly Jews. He remembered his ancestry. He knew his place and was willing to take it. Did he lose by doing this? Not in comparison with what he gained!

God warned in Jeremiah 45:5: "And seekest thou great things for thyself? seek them not." This is not a rebuke to legitimate ambition. We must keep our balance and maintain our perspective. There are times when our desires have to be laid aside for the well-being of others. Willingness to do this is a real indication of humility.

In our self-centered world success is everything. Anything else is secondary. A relentless urge drives many toward the pinnacle of success. Humility is forgotten in the ruthless quest for fame.

This is not God's way. The way up is *down*. Serving others is the highest goal of life. Such an attitude gives one a new set of values. No greater satisfaction can be enjoyed than the kind that comes in service. Jesus declared that He did not come to be ministered to, but to minister. This is what He was teaching when He washed the disciples' feet at the Last Supper. He was their Master, but He was doing what a household slave did when guests came.

Here's a good verse to think about at this point: "The fear of the Lord is the instruction of wisdom; and before honor is humility" (Proverbs 15:33).

There are so many lessons all around us to warn us against adopting the world's philosophy. How many have you known who exhausted themselves in pursuit of personal success they never got to enjoy? Even if they reached their goal, such a philosophy produces spiritual blindness. It often robs one of genuine compassion. It's terribly unhealthy to have all our thoughts turned inward.

Try this on for size: "But the meek shall inherit the earth; and shall delight themselves in the abundance of peace" (Psalm 37:11). Jesus endorsed this in His Sermon on the Mount. We could properly insert *humble* for "meek," for this is the meaning.

Admit Your Need

"Blessed are the poor in spirit: for theirs is the kingdom of heaven" (Matthew 5:3). The "poor in spirit" are those who recognize they are spiritually bankrupt apart from God's grace. They confess that without the Lord they are nothing. What about people with a proud, haughty spirit? What about that fellow who refuses to acknowledge his own insufficiency? He will receive absolutely nothing from God. The path to Him is the path of humility. "Nothing in my hand I bring"—that's the road to travel.

Our reaction to God's spiritual demands will determine how willing we are to serve others. Instead of trying to dodge the Word let's receive it, apply it, and obey it. We have to get rid of all sham, make-believe, pretense, and subterfuge. Instead of excusing our behavior, let's find the true reason for it. Then we must deal with it.

When we have admitted to the Lord our need and received His help, we are in a position to help others. Humbling ourselves is good for our ego. Most of us have an abundant supply of the latter. It will yell loudly when it is pinched. But we can't let that stop us. The question is, "Do we want God's best?" If we do, the way to receive it is very plain.

Go Down to Go Up

A humble person is willing to accept the lowest place. This isn't the world's recipe for success, but it's God's. Human nature seeks the position that is most glamorous. If it brings lots of recognition that's what the old ego craves. But God's way is the reverse. He says the way up is down. The Scriptures promise that if we humble ourselves we will be exalted. They also warn that if we exalt ourselves we will be brought down.

Everything the world considers success is *not* success! Many who are great in God's sight are completely unnoticed by others. Whose approval are we after—the world's or God's? The world's applause soon dies. It may even turn to "boos." But to have the smile of God is to have a reward that is eternal.

Listen to the wise words of Proverbs 25:6,7: "Put not forth thyself in the presence of the king, and stand not in the place of great men: for better it is that it be said unto thee, Come up hither; than that thou shouldest be put lower in the presence of the prince whom thine eyes have seen."

Are we really willing to take the lowest place? Can we go to the camp meeting and be an usher? or pick up the paper on the grounds? or tend the tents? It may seem more glamorous to be leading the singing, but your place may be frying hamburgers after the service is over.

Here is a plain, simple rule for the kind of living that pleases the Lord: "What doth the Lord require of thee, but to do justly, and to love mercy, and to walk humbly with thy God" (Micah 6:8).

And here is another lesson from the greatest Teacher of all: "And Jesus called a little child unto him, and set him in the midst of them, and said, Verily I say unto you, Except ye be converted, and become as little children, ye shall not enter into the kingdom of heaven. Whosoever therefore shall humble himself as this little child, the same is greatest in the kingdom of heaven" (Matthew 18:2-4).

That sounds strange because it's so completely opposite to the world's philosophy. But who cares? The world's attitude has always run contrary to God's will. Just don't forget where the world's philosophy will take you in the end!

Too often the person who exalts himself does it at the expense of others. He does not care who he tramples in his climb. But the day will come when others will trample him. You can't violate God's rules without paying the penalty.

The Perfect Pattern

The Lord Jesus is our great and perfect Pattern. Before He came to earth He was at the Father's right hand. Sinful humanity demanded a Redeemer. Jesus was the only One who could do it. It meant terrible humiliation. He had to step from His throne to this evil world. It was like walking from your nice clean home to the city dump—only much worse.

While He lived here Jesus was subject to all the things that beset us. He was weary and hungry. He shed tears. He suffered. Why? Because He loves us. Are we willing to exercise a little humility to show our love for another?

Here's the way Philippians 2:5-9 describes our Saviour's great self-humbling: "Let this mind be in you, which was also in Christ Jesus: who, being in the form of God, thought it not robbery to be equal with God: but made himself of no reputation, and took upon him the form of a servant, and was made in the likeness of men: and being found in fashion as a man, he humbled himself, and became obedient unto death, even the death of the cross. Wherefore God also hath highly exalted him, and given him a name which is above every name." The pattern couldn't be plainer. Are we willing to follow it?

Look at some of the things Jesus gave up so He could save us:

1. Position—This means a lot to us, doesn't it? Human nature clings to its position of prominence with a vengeance. Christ gave up His position at the Father's right hand to become a babe in a manger. The position one holds doesn't always indicate greatness of character. Some are chained to circumstances that obscure them, but this doesn't keep them from developing character. When advancement comes we must be careful to keep a true estimate of ourselves. Any kind of promotion must not make us vain and foolishly proud.

2. Power—It's easy to abuse power. Satan tried to get Jesus to do it. The temptation to turn stones into bread was the devil's way of persuading our Lord to use His power selfishly. He was goading Him to use it fanatically by jumping off the temple. Of course, Jesus said a firm "No" to every satanic suggestion. He had the power to do these things, but He refused to exercise it. To have done so would have made it impossible for Him to become our Redeemer.

3. Pride—A few words of praise are fatal to some people. We must be constantly on guard against pride becoming our downfall. There was no false pride in Christ. He didn't keep saying, "I'm God's Son, so I can do as I please." Instead He constantly submitted His will to the Father's. That's true humility.

Deeds, Not Just Words

It's easy to talk about humility, but Jesus did more than that. His act of washing the disciples' feet was a powerful example of humility in action. Of course His greatest demonstration was when He went to the cross. Are we as willing to take up our cross and to keep it when our enemies jeer?

Every Christian must face the question: "Will I serve or try to *be* served?" The attitude of serving has practically disappeared from our world. Everyone wants to "get" instead of "give." This philosophy is completely anti-Christian.

Jesus told of two men who went to the temple to pray. One was a Pharisee. He considered himself a very holy man. In his prayer he reminded God of all the wonderful things he had done. He had no real sense of spiritual need. All he wanted to do was impress the Lord with his goodness.

The other man was a tax collector. Nobody had to tell him he was a sinner. He knew it. When he prayed he didn't even lift up his eyes. He felt completely unworthy to even look toward heaven. He simply hit himself on the chest and cried, "God be merciful to me, a sinner." Jesus declared that of the two who went to pray, only one was right with God when he got home. He was the tax collector. His humility won him favor with God. The pride of the Pharisee brought him condemnation.

Listen to Paul's good advice: "For I say, through the grace given unto me, to every man that is among you, not to think of himself more highly than he ought to think; but to think soberly, according as God hath dealt to every man the measure of faith" (Romans 12:3). That really doesn't need any explanation, does it? It defines humility very well.

There Are Rewards

The Bible is full of promises to the humble. We We read in 1 Peter 5:5,6: "Likewise, ye younger, submit yourselves unto the elder. Yea, all of you be subject one to another, and be clothed with humility: for God resisteth the proud, and giveth grace to the humble. Humble yourselves therefore under the mighty hand of God, that he may exalt you in due time."

Humbling yourself isn't so hard if you consider that you are doing it as to the Lord—"under the mighty hand of God." Did you notice that expression "clothed with humility"? There is no better taste in clothing than this!

The one who has the right estimate of himself will always be able to see life in its true perspective. He will escape the snares that await the proud and haughty. Being thoroughly teachable, he will learn many lessons others miss. He will walk with God and become acquainted with mysteries hidden to others.

The humble person is spared the strain of constantly trying to prove how great he is. If compliments or advancements come he will enjoy them much more than if he exhausted himself trying to attain them.

Humility brings a blessed relaxation to one's spirit. Humble pie never tastes as bad as the devil tries to make you think!

9 Learn to Say "Thank You"

Gratitude is one's response to kindness. It is the attitude of being appreciative and thankful. If we sometimes don't feel grateful it's because we just haven't taken time to count our blessings. We should spend more time thanking God for His blessings and less time asking for more. Try it—you'll like it!

Gratitude in the home is important, too. It's easy to take for granted the things we enjoy in our family circle and never say, "'Thank you." In fact, there isn't any area of life that can't be helped by frequent "thank yous" and extra gratitude.

The Psalmist complained: "And they have rewarded me evil for good, and hatred for my love" (Psalm 109:5). That's tough to take, isn't it? Let's be sure we don't respond that way to people's kindness.

Remember the 10 lepers Jesus healed? The story is recorded in Luke 17:11-19. Naturally they had to keep their distance, as lepers in those days always did. But they shouted loudly enough for Jesus to hear them clearly. "Jesus, Master, have mercy on us," was their plea. Jesus told them to go to the priest for examination in accordance with the Mosaic law. The record of the miracle is short and beautiful: "And it came to pass, that, as they went, they were cleansed."

You would expect a loud outpouring of gratitude from all 10, wouldn't you? Strangely enough, this wasn't the case. One of them came back to thank Jesus with a loud voice. He was so grateful he even fell on his face at Jesus' feet. There must have been real sorrow in Jesus' question: "Were there not ten cleansed? but where are the nine?"

How often must the Lord ask this question today? So many have been blessed; and a few cry, "Thank you, Lord!" But where are the others?

Count Your Blessings

First, let's keep thanking the Lord for our salvation, no matter how long we have been saved. The Psalmist cried out: "Oh that men would praise the Lord for his goodness, and for his wonderful works to the children of men!" (Psalm 107:15). Of all God's works, none is greater than saving and cleansing a sinful soul.

Let's never take our salvation for granted. Where would you be if the Holy Spirit had never convicted you of your sin and brought you to Christ? Paul declared: "By the grace of God I am what I am" (1 Corinthians 15:10). We can all echo the same truth.

"Oh give thanks unto the Lord; for he is good: because his mercy endureth for ever" (Psalm 118:1). Have you thanked God for His mercy lately?

Listen to what Paul wrote to the Colossians: "Giving thanks unto the Father, which hath made us meet to be partakers of the inheritance of the saints in light" (1:12). "Rooted and built up in him, and stablished in the faith, as ye have been taught, abounding therein with thanksgiving" (2:7).

Our salvation brings blessing to us in two worlds —this one and the next. Through Christ we have everlasting life. We have a heavenly home waiting for us. But even in this life there are rewards. Can we ever thank God enough for the peace, joy, and contentment that come as a direct result of our trust in Christ?

The Christian can pillow his head at night in peace. He enjoys a clear conscience. These are things you don't find in the unbelieving crowd. Christ has delivered us from our fears. He has given life a new direction. He has given us freedom from self, Satan, and the world. Thank you, Jesus!

Paul told the Thessalonians that he thanked God without ceasing for their salvation (1 Thessalonians 2:13). Are we as ceaseless in our thanks for our own salvation?

Christian Friends

To the Philippians Paul wrote: "I thank my God upon every remembrance of you" (Philippians 1:3). The memory of their friendship sustained the apostle in his prison cell. What would we do without Christian friends? How often do we thank God for them? None of us can stand alone; we need others. How often we would give up the fight if there weren't a friend to encourage us.

Sometimes our best friends are the ones we take for granted. They are always there, so we may forget what it would be like if they weren't. To our shame we must confess that those who do the most for us often receive our worst treatment. Let's stop and take a fresh look at our friends and what they mean to us. After that, how about a telephone call, a letter, or a personal visit to say, "Thank you for what you have meant to me."

Fellowship

"I thank my God . . . for your fellowship in the gospel from the very first day until now" (Philippians 1:3,5).

Fellowship is a word often heard in Christian circles. Our experience with the Lord is made more precious by the fact that we share it with others.

Have you ever been in a situation where fellowship was denied you for a while? Is there anything more uncomfortable for a Christian? Much of our communion with the Lord takes place in private. But there is a place for united worship, and this must never be left out. The Church is a fellowship. Thank God for it.

All Other Things

Where can we find a stopping place when we try to name all the things we are thankful for? Paul sums it up in Ephesians 5:20 by saying: "Giving thanks always for *all things* unto God and the Father in the name of our Lord Jesus Christ."

This certainly includes the blessing of good health. It includes the blessing of good food on the table. (Do you return thanks before each meal?) It includes the privilege of living in a free land like America. We should be grateful for our church, our family, and, in short, for everything.

It's in order to thank God for the sunlight, the rain, and the air we breathe. Let's stop to thank Him for the beauty we see around us in nature.

Did you ever thank God for accidents that don't happen? Traveling on the highway is dangerous, and many accidents occur. When we arrive home safely from a trip we should look up and give thanks to our Father who watches over us.

It's a Sin

Ingratitude is a sin. Israel's history in the Old Testament is an endless account of ingratitude. Each time those people backslid they seemed to lose all sense of appreciation for their blessings. Through Isaiah God delivered this rebuke: "The ox knoweth his owner, and the ass his master's crib: but Israel doth not know, my people doth not consider" (Isaiah 1:3). In other words, the animals of the farm knew where to go for their food and were thankful for it, but not Israel. They were inferior to beasts in their sense of gratitude.

Joseph felt the sting of ingratitude while he was in prison. He befriended the butler, who was a fellow prisoner. For this favor the butler promised to bring Joseph's case to Pharaoh's attention when he was released. But he forgot about it when he got his freedom. Joseph, of course, stayed in jail, wondering why he had been so ill-treated.

How many have been healed of serious illnesses but never show their thanks to God by living for Him? Sometimes they cry and pray and promise all kinds of things while they are suffering. But often these vows are forgotten when the blessing of health returns. If this isn't a sin, what is?

David was a blessing to King Saul. He played his harp for the king during the king's times of mental depression. He killed Goliath and thus defeated the Philistines when everyone else was afraid. Despite all this, Saul rewarded David by trying to kill him. For a long time he hunted him like a common criminal.

Paul sacrificed much for the church at Corinth. But the day came when the Corinthians listened to false apostles who slandered Paul and tried to undermine his influence. Some of God's ministers today have been treated in similar fashion by those they have tried to help.

Ingratitude can be shown by an employee who fails to appreciate the privilege of having a job and doesn't give his best for the pay he receives. Did you ever hear someone joke about "backing up to the window to get his pay" because he knew he had not done his best?

But home is the place where ingratitude probably shows itself the most. For some reason we are often the least appreciative of those we love. It will gladden the heart of your loved ones to tell them often that you appreciate them. There is no one in this world who does not appreciate being thanked—the schoolteacher, the minister, the paper boy. Even YOU like to be patted on the back once in a while, don't you?

How to Stay on Top

Ingratitude from others can get you down pretty quickly. Nothing is more discouraging than to do your best to treat people right and then get the opposite treatment from them.

What do you do when this happens? Is it possible to get the victory over ingratitude? Yes, if you're determined. First, pray. Don't pray once or twice. Keep it up until you know you're on top. That's what David did. Listen: "They rewarded me evil for good to the spoiling of my soul. But as for me, when they were sick, my clothing was sackcloth: I humbled my soul with fasting; and my prayer returned into mine own bosom" (Psalm 35:12,13).

In other words, instead of gloating over his enemies' misfortune David prayed for them. This has always been the surest path to victory. Don't let the other fellow's ingratitude embitter your own soul. You're the loser if you do. And you haven't helped him.

Isn't this what Jesus practiced? On the cross He prayed for God to forgive those who crucified Him. The first Christian martyr, Stephen, prayed for his murderers with his dying breath. How much better this was than to die cursing them or praying judgment on them. Stephen was portraying the true spirit of his Lord.

You can do a lot to win the victory by your own faithfulness. The very weight of faithful acts often overcomes ingratitude. Returning good for evil can make the offender ashamed. Sometimes it seems that trying to do the right thing brings no reward. This isn't so. The constant faithful effort pays off. Someone will recognize your record and honor you for it. Don't let the ingrate drag you down to his level! Never try to pay back ingratitude with more of the same. It will simply make the whole thing snowball, and it will hurt your own spirit. Revenge accomplishes nothing.

Paul faced this very thing with the Corinthian church. Here's how he handled it: "And I will very gladly spend and be spent for you; though the more abundantly I love you, the less I be loved" (2 Corinthians 12:15). To love and keep on loving when love is not returned is hard. But eventually it bears fruit. The eyes of the ungrateful can be opened by persevering love when they are blind to everything else.

This may be a bit on the negative side, but the knowledge that ingratitude will be punished is a comfort. We don't have to punish the unthankful; God will take care of it. Proverbs 17:13 puts the proposition very plainly: "Whoso rewardeth evil for good, evil shall not depart from his house."

A Precious Jewel

Like a precious jewel, gratitude never loses its value. Its worth increases with the passing of time. Colossians 3:17 admonishes us: "And whatsoever ye do in word or deed, do all in the name of the Lord Jesus, giving thanks to God and the Father by him." This makes it clear that gratitude should permeate the Christian life in its entirety. A grateful spirit enhances character, helps the disposition, and makes us a blessing to others.

Being thankful to God will help us turn all we do into acts of worship. Menial tasks lose their monotony when we see them as part of our day's service done in the Lord's name.

In 2 Samuel 9 we read of a noble act of David after he became king. Usually kings tried to get rid of the relatives of their predecessors. But David began searching for Saul's relatives so he might show them kindness "for Jonathan's sake."

Jonathan was Saul's son, but, unlike his father, he was David's devoted friend. When Saul tried to kill David, Jonathan befriended him. David did not forget. When he finally ascended the throne Jonathan had been killed in battle. It would have been easy for David to reason, "Jonathan's gone. There's no point in feeling obligated to any of his family." But David was a man after God's own heart. Gratitude was ingrained in his nature.

Remember the women who went to Jesus' tomb on that first Easter morning? The last thing they expected was His resurrection. They went to anoint His body with spices. It was all they knew to do to show honor to Him now that He was dead. Jesus had been such a blessing to them. This was their way of showing their gratitude. These women knew their Lord's followers were in the minority. They had felt the sting of hatred from many. But this did not deter them from taking their stand for their Lord. Nothing could stop them from expressing their thanks even after He had been crucified.

The Early Church was permeated with a spirit of gratitude. The spiritual condition of those Christians is expressed in the words of Acts 2:47: "Praising God, and having favor with all the people." No wonder the latter part of this verse says: "And the Lord added to the church daily such as should be saved." A spirit of thanksgiving promotes revival.

Peace of mind is linked with gratitude in Colossians 3:15: "And let the peace of God rule in your hearts, to the which also ye are called in one body; and be ye thankful."

It says a lot for the spiritual background of our nation that we have a national holiday called "Thanksgiving." To some it may have lost its meaning, but its annual recurrence is still a reminder that we have much to be grateful for. The message of the day may get through to some who might otherwise not stop to give thanks.

Try saying "thank you" more. You'll be happily surprised at what it does for you.

10 Old Faithful

The most famous geyser in Yellowstone National Park is "Old Faithful." It got its nickname because it is so dependable. You can count on it to erupt at very regular intervals. Wouldn't it be great to have a church full of "old faithfuls"? Thank God, there are a few! They are so dependable that if they are once given an assignment, no one has to worry about it being done. Unfortunately, their numbers are not large.

"A faithful man who can find?" That question was asked a long time ago. It is recorded in Proverbs 20:6. Many a Christian leader has probably asked it since then.

Simply defined, *faithfulness* is conscientiousness in performing duty. It means trustworthiness; dependability; steadfastness. It's a trait God wants to find in every Christian.

"There shall be showers of blessing." How we love to sing it! But the Christian life is one of responsibility as well as blessing. A real test of character is our reaction to responsibility. God wants people who are loyal and dependable. There are big loads to carry in the Lord's work and there is always a need for faithful Christians.

We may be loaded with talent, but if we won't stick to the job the church suffers. It isn't enough to stay ahead during three quarters of the game. The final score depends on what we do in the last quarter. The runner can't quit until he crosses the finish line. God wants winners. We can be one of them if we will keep everlastingly at our spiritual tasks.

We're talking about faithfulness in small tasks as well as big ones. When we give a good performance in our Christian race the effect is widespread. Many are watching—saved and unsaved. Our faithfulness will impress and encourage many who might otherwise falter.

Jesus commanded: "Continue ye in my love" (John 15:9). Through Jude's pen the Holy Spirit tells us: "But ye, beloved, building up yourselves on your most holy faith . . ." (Jude 20). That's faithfulness—continuing; building up. There is no stopping place. We must keep going on. Just because we've been faithful for a long time we can't take a vacation. Our commitment must be never-ending. We just can't entertain any thoughts of ever letting down.

Faithfulness to God

At some time in his life every Christian faces a test of his loyalty to God. Daniel is an outstanding example of one who passed the test with flying colors. Here's a brief account of his experience:

"Then the presidents and princes sought to find occasion against Daniel concerning the kingdom; but they could find none occasion nor fault; forasmuch as he was faithful, neither was there any error or fault found in him. Then said these men, We shall not find any occasion against this Daniel, except we find it against him concerning the law of his God. . . .

"Now when Daniel knew that the writing was signed, he went into his house; and, his windows being open in his chamber toward Jerusalem, he kneeled upon his knees three times a day, and prayed, and gave thanks before his God, as he did aforetime" (Daniel 6:4,5,10).

Daniel had the good habit of praying three times a day. His enemies tried to turn this faithfulness into a trap. With great subtlety they induced the king to make a law that no one could pray to anyone but him. The penalty for disobedience was death.

Daniel heard the news very quickly. What would you or I have done? Daniel preferred death to giving up his prayer life. When his enemies followed him to his house they weren't surprised. They found him doing what he had always done. Three times a day he opened his windows toward Jerusalem and knelt to pray. Communion with God was more important to him than life itself. Compromise would have been easy, but Daniel didn't even think of it.

How wonderful if every Christian were this concerned about his walk with the Lord. Little things come between God and us so easily. Prayer gets crowded out. Bible reading is the last thing on our schedule. Many professing Christians need little excuse to miss church. Can it be they haven't learned that obligations go with blessings? There is more to the Christian life than enjoying the good things of the Lord. There's work to be done, and few to do it.

And who hasn't heard of Daniel's three friends? Shadrach, Meshach, and Abednego had big government jobs. But one day they had to choose between loyalty to the king and loyalty to God. Nebuchadnezzar had set up a great image that everyone was supposed to worship. These three wouldn't bow, so into the furnace they went. But God didn't let them burn. He rewarded their faithfulness by delivering them. But they had already declared that even if God didn't deliver them they still would be true to Him (Daniel 3). That kind of faithfulness will *always* stand the fire!

It Must Begin at Home

It's amazing how much teaching the Bible has about the home. Paul wrote to the Ephesians:

"Wives, submit yourselves unto your own husbands, as unto the Lord. . . . Husbands, love your wives, even as Christ also loved the church and gave himself for it; . . . Children, obey your parents in the Lord: for this is right. Honor thy father and mother; which is the first commandment with promise" (5:22,25; 6:1,2).

You'll never find better rules in any man's book. The Bible is the best book in the world on marriage counseling and child raising. Too bad it's ignored so often!

The pressures of modern living have been tough on the home. The spirit of the age has devastated the stability of the family. If we're to have a better world we must have better homes. Each member of the family can't go his separate way. The responsibility doesn't rest on one or two, but on all. Parents must be faithful to each other and to their children. In return, children must show love, loyalty, and obedience to dad and mom. Each one must have the welfare of the whole family at heart. If he pursues his own selfish aims there's trouble ahead.

If you want happiness, peacefulness, and serenity in the family, start with the basics. When Christ is the Head of the home He makes a difference. Prayer and Bible study will change the whole atmosphere within those four walls. Call it a family altar, devotions, quiet time, or anything else you like. Just be sure it happens—every day.

Family members must be true to their obligations to each other. If one makes a promise to another, it should be kept. Confidence and trust are developed when people keep their word. It doesn't have to be broken often for mistrust to creep in.

Home responsibilities should be divided. The load shouldn't fall on one or two. When assignments are given there should be no question about them being carried out. This is faithfulness.

The Bible emphasizes the authority of the husband. Obviously this does not give him license to be a tyrant. He is to love and cherish his wife and treat her with great consideration. She must not resent the scriptural command to submit to her husband's authority. If that authority is exercised in love, the chances are she won't harbor bitter feelings about it. The Bible does have a plan of home government. Everyone has his place. When it is faithfully filled, home will be like heaven.

When the Doors Are Open, Be There!

If the Bible speaks loudly on any subject it's our faithfulness to church. Let's look at Hebrews 10:19-25:

"Having therefore, brethren, boldness to enter into the holiest by the blood of Jesus, by a new and living way, which he hath consecrated for us, through the veil, that is to say, his flesh; and having a high priest over the house of God; let us draw near with a true heart in full assurance of faith, having our hearts sprinkled from an evil conscience, and our bodies washed with pure water. Let us hold fast the profession of our faith without wavering; for he is faithful that promised; and let us consider one another to provoke unto love and to good works: not forsaking the assembling of ourselves together, as the manner of some is; but exhorting one another: and so much the more, as ye see the day approaching."

Why have so many forgotten their responsibility to God's house? Sunday is a holiday instead of a holy day to many. It's visiting day, hunting day, fishing day, swimming day—everything but the Lord's Day. On a national average less than 40 percent of all Americans attend church on Sunday morning. Is it any wonder our nation is so bewildered and confused?

Faithful church attendance isn't something a Christian can take or leave. Talk about a duty or obligation —this is it! We owe a portion of our time to God and His house. Worship is a responsibility we can't rightfully shirk.

It's true that life is more complicated today. It's also obvious that improved transportation makes it much easier for people to get places faster. This gives us much more leisure time. Unfortunately, this can be a curse as well as a blessing. Spiritually, our leisure madness is dragging us down. There is a national mania for pleasure.

Christians must resist this terrible pull. Paul admonished Timothy: "Continue thou in the things which thou hast learned and hast been assured of, . . . that the man of God may be perfect, thoroughly furnished unto all good works" (2 Timothy 3:14,17).

There is no question that the reestablishment of a strong religious life in our country would make our problems more solvable. If every person attended the services of his church every week a spiritual awakening could take place across the whole land. Let's be the leaders in this kind of movement. There's great power in example.

Start With Little Things

"He that is faithful in that which is least is faithful also in much: and he that is unjust in the least is unjust also in much. If therefore ye have not been faithful in the unrighteous mammon, who will commit to your trust the true riches? And if ye have not been faithful in that which is another man's, who shall give you that which is your own?" (Luke 16:10-12).

"Moreover it is required in stewards, that a man be found faithful" (1 Corinthians 4:2).

Sometimes folks complain that an important position has not been given them, when they have not been dependable in small tasks. If we can't be faithful at home we won't be faithful on the mission field. There is no point in asking God to send us to some far-off place if we can't stay on the job at home.

Every small duty that comes our way is a test. If we do the small job faithfully it fits us for something bigger. We have to step on the first rung of the ladder before we can reach the top.

Paul compared the Church to a human body. Think of all the parts of the body, both large and small. If even the little finger doesn't perform right it affects the whole physical being. You may think you're the least member of the Church, but if you let down on your job the program will be adversely affected.

A boy got a job at a large hardware store. His first assignment was in the attic. His boss showed him a box full of nails and screws of all sizes. There were hinges, old tools, and bits of iron. He was told to put it all in order.

The attic was gloomy and dusty. The work seemed useless and tiresome. Nobody was watching him, and he was tempted to take a nap. But instead he made up his mind to do his work well. He made compartments in the box and sorted out the articles carefully. It took 3 days.

When the head clerk inspected the work he told the young man, "You will be given a place at my counter. That box is a test job we give to see whether a boy will be worthy of a better place."

Isn't every duty in life a test job? If we do it right we're better able to tackle something more difficult. Don't be ashamed of the small tasks. Do them well. Learn all you can about your job. Apply yourself faithfully. Someone is sure to observe your actions, and promotion will come in due time.

Be sure to carry this attitude into your work in the church. If you're supposed to clean the floors and the washrooms, make them sparkle. If you're a Sunday school teacher give your class your very best. Prepare well for it, teach faithfully, and God will reward you. Maybe you're on the visitation committee. Don't give up when only a few turn out to visit. Keep faithfully at the task. You won't lose your reward.

God Is Watching

Colossians 3:23 tells us: "And whatsoever ye do, do it heartily, as to the Lord, and not unto men." Never forget that you are working as unto the Lord. If men don't always recognize you, commit your disappointment to God. He'll take care of the payoff.

Remember the Parable of the Talents in Matthew 25:14-30? The man with five talents gained five more. The two-talent man gained two more. The one who had only one talent didn't bother to try increasing it. He buried it and forgot about it until his master returned.

Remember the master's words to the faithful servants? "Well done, good and faithful servant; thou hast been faithful over a few things, I will make thee ruler over many things: enter thou into the joy of thy lord" (v. 23).

But don't forget how he rebuked the fellow who did nothing with his talent: "Thou wicked and slothful servant, thou knewest that I reap where I sowed not, and gather where I have not strewed: . . . Take therefore the talent from him. . . . And cast ye the unprofitable servant into outer darkness: there shall be weeping and gnashing of teeth" (vv. 26,28,30).

Faithfulness to Friends

Proverbs 11:13 says: "A talebearer revealeth secrets: but he that is of a faithful spirit concealeth the matter." Everyone needs a friend like this—someone who will help shield us from criticism, hide our faults from others, and encourage us when we are downcast.

If your friend confides in you don't betray his secret. Maybe it's a choice bit of gossip, but you're unfaithful if you tell it. Everyone has to unburden himself at times. You should consider it an honor to be chosen as a confidant.

If a friend is in need let's help him to the best of our ability. Someday the shoe may be on the other foot. *We* may be the one needing help. It will be comforting then to know that we have sown our own seeds of kindness. "Fair-weather friends" are a dime a dozen. A *faithful* friend is a precious jewel.

11 Take Time to Be Holy

A real Christian is a brand-new person. Jesus called salvation a new birth. Paul wrote in 2 Corinthians 5:17: "Therefore if any man be in Christ, he is a new creature: old things are passed away; behold, all things are become new."

Salvation is supernatural. It's the work of God. When we are saved God's own nature is implanted in us. A miracle? Exactly! And it's a miracle that affects the whole life. No part is left out—actions, thoughts, words, attitudes, affections, and associations. You can sum it up in one word—*holiness*.

Holiness has its negative aspect. There are things a holy person doesn't do. But holiness is also a positive attribute of character. Besides refraining from acts of sin the holy person performs acts of righteousness. Not only does he hate the things that are wrong, he loves God and diligently pursues that which is good and upright. He turns the throne room of his heart over to the Lord Jesus to rule and reign.

We cannot sit idly by and obtain holiness. It comes through action—through doing, seeking, and serving.

Here's what the writer to the Hebrews said:

"Furthermore, we have had fathers of our flesh which corrected us, and we gave them reverence: shall we not much rather be in subjection unto the Father of spirits, and live? For they verily for a few days chastened us after their own pleasure; but he for our profit, that we might be partakers of his holiness. Now no chastening for the present seemeth to be joyous, but grievous: nevertheless, afterward it yieldeth the peaceable fruit of righteousness unto them which are exercised thereby.

"Wherefore lift up the hands which hang down, and the feeble knees; and make straight paths for your feet, lest that which is lame be turned out of the way; but let it rather be healed. Follow peace with all men, and holiness, without which no man shall see the Lord" (Hebrews 12:9-14).

God's heart yearns for a pure people who love Him. His Word tells us we are called to be "saints," or holy ones. This means we must be separated from the sins of the present age. Our dedication must be to God and His service.

Holy comes from an old Anglo-Saxon word meaning "whole; well." No one can be a whole person unless he lives according to God's will. He cannot be spiritually healthy unless he is holy. Never forget this: God means for holiness to be the rule of the Christian life; not the exception.

Start With the Mind

"'Let us cleanse ourselves from all filthiness of the flesh and spirit, perfecting holiness in the fear of God" (2 Corinthians 7:1).

"Though we walk in the flesh, we do not war after the flesh" (10:3).

"Casting down imaginations, and every high thing that exalteth itself against the knowledge of God, and bringing into captivity every thought to the obedience of Christ" (v. 5).

All deeds begin with thoughts. The mind is the seedbed of all actions. The brain is the nerve center of the whole life. Thus the battle against sin must be won first in the thought life.

No wonder the mind is a battleground between God and Satan. The one who controls the mind controls the person. Whatever we do, we must not be careless about our thoughts. It's easier to discipline ourselves physically than mentally. But we must discipline our minds if we are concerned with holiness.

The people of Noah's day were so wicked God had to destroy them. Here is the Biblical indictment of that generation: "And God saw that the wickedness of man was great in the earth, and that every imagination of the thoughts of his heart was only evil continually" (Genesis 6:5). Notice the emphasis on the evil minds of those people. Because their thoughts were corrupt their deeds were the same.

What are evil thoughts? We face a constant inner conflict. Paul says our "old man" wants to rule us. Every evil thing in the world finds easy access to the human mind. Satan is an expert at infiltrating our brains at every opportunity. If he sees a sign of weakness he leaps to the attack. Naturally he anticipates a breakdown that will destroy us spiritually.

Think of the opportunity for planting evil thoughts in our minds today. Never has there been such mass communication. We have TV, radio, movies, magazines, newspapers, comic books, pamphlets, and so on.

This constant barrage of Satan's missiles is affecting the thought life of our whole nation. Sales of pornography have reached new heights. Music that appeals to the lowest instincts blares out everywhere. The ever-increasing divorce rate is fed by the glamorized lives of Hollywood's many-times-married movie stars. The liquor industry cleverly suggests that drinking is a social grace. The repetition of these evil appeals is incessant. Is it any wonder that our land is going downhill morally?

Fill Your Mind With Good

When the Pharisees criticized Jesus and His disciples for not washing their hands before eating, Jesus answered with some great teaching. He reminded those folks that a man is not defiled by what goes into him, but what comes out. He named specific evils and declared that they are the result of uncleanness within: "For out of the heart proceed evil thoughts, murders, adulteries, fornications, thefts, false witness, blasphemies" (Matthew 15:19).

Filling our mind with good thoughts is the best way to keep out bad thoughts. Spend lots of time meditating on the Bible. The Word has a holy influence. It will soon permeate your mind and counteract thoughts of sin and impurity. Prayer is like a mental detergent. It will cleanse the mind and fill it with thoughts of God and righteousness.

Be careful what you read. There is wholesome literature besides the Bible that Christians can read profitably. But there's a lot of the other kind, too. Many of today's best-sellers have a strong sex emphasis. A Christian can't afford to give them any attention. Even respectable magazines sometimes stoop to carry articles that smack of vulgarity. And be sure to keep that TV under control! Never has there been such a need to screen the programs we watch. The same goes for the radio.

When we're alone with time on our hands we must really be on guard. It was at such a time that King David committed his terrible sin of adultery with Bathsheba. You've heard that "an idle mind is the devil's workshop." This isn't a Biblical quotation, but it's true.

Here's Paul's formula for maintaining a holy thought life: "Finally, brethren, whatsoever things are true, whatsoever things are honest, whatsoever things are just, whatsoever things are pure, whatsoever things are lovely, whatsoever things are of good report; if there be any virtue, and if there be any praise, *think* on these things" (Philippians 4:8).

Try to follow these rules: (1) Banish all wrong thoughts as soon as they present themselves. (2) Turn your thoughts to right things. (3) Repeat your good thoughts. Bring them before your mind again and again.

Accept no compromise with yourself when it comes to evil thoughts. Be a stern disciplinarian of your thinking. God's grace will help you.

Watch That Tongue!

No stronger words were ever written about the tongue than these:

"And the tongue is a fire, a world of iniquity: so is the tongue among our members, that it defileth the whole body, and setteth on fire the course of nature; and it is set on fire of hell. For every kind of beasts, and of birds, and of serpents, and of things in the sea, is tamed, and hath been tamed of mankind:

but the tongue can no man tame; it is an unruly evil, full of deadly poison" (James 3:6-8).

Can you really be holy if your speech isn't holy? Hardly. It's easy to be careless in our conversation. The Christian has to be on guard constantly when he's talking. Certainly he must leave vulgarity, profanity, and coarse slang out of his speech. Irreverence must be shunned. It is never becoming to make jokes of sacred things. Spiritual matters should not be spoken of lightly.

Some Christians who would not think of swearing, sometimes use the Lord's name in a way that is actually "in vain." When His name is on our lips we should always be sure it is used in sincerity and reverence.

James has more to say about the tongue: "For in many things we offend all. If any man offend not in word, the same is a perfect man, and able also to bridle the whole body" (James 3:2). In other words, if a man can control his speech he will be able to control every other aspect of his life.

It's so easy to offend with our speech. A careless word can cut like a knife. The scar may never heal. An ancient wise man said, "Think twice before you speak once." A modern version is: "Be sure brain is engaged before mouth is set in motion!"

Of course, for a holy person gossip is out! It may be great entertainment to criticize others, but it's terribly unwholesome. It's tragic, but some churches have been divided and hindered because of a long tongue. Friendships have been broken because someone said the wrong thing.

Of course, lying is out of the question for a child of God. So is exaggerating, or so-called "stretching the truth." Don't forget that excessive flattery can become outright lying.

Jesus had a very stern warning in Matthew 12:36, 37: "But I say unto you, That every idle word that men shall speak, they shall give account thereof in the day of judgment. For by thy words thou shalt be justified, and by thy words thou shalt be condemned." Maybe we ought to paste these words where we'll see them every morning.

"All Manner of Conversation"

Let's look at two passages from Peter's writings:

"As obedient children, not fashioning yourselves according to the former lusts in your ignorance: but as he which hath called you is holy, so be ye holy in all manner of conversation; because it is written, Be ye holy; for I am holy" (1 Peter 1:14-16).

"Seeing then that all these things shall be dissolved, what manner of persons ought ye to be in all holy conversation and godliness . . . ?" (2 Peter 3:11).

When we are tempted to turn our tongue loose, let's remember that the Lord is coming soon. Do we want to be talking like that when He returns?

Words are powerful. They can bless, and when used for evil purposes they can destroy. Listen to Paul's teaching:

"But now ye also put off all these; anger, wrath, malice, blasphemy, filthy communication out of your mouth" (Colossians 3:8).

"Let no corrupt communication proceed out of your mouth" (Ephesians 4:29).

James is very plain, too: "But above all things, my brethren, swear not, neither by heaven, neither by the earth, neither by any other oath" (James 5:12).

Deeds Count, Too

"Let your light so shine before men, that they may see your good works, and glorify your Father which is in heaven." Those are Jesus' words in Matthew 5:16. Men *do* see us. The thing they see is our works. Good deeds are important in the Christian life. In James' epistle he teaches that the world can see our faith only by our works.

The Bible is full of teaching about the works of Christians. Paul told Titus to "exhort servants to be obedient unto their own masters, and to please them well in all things" (Titus 2:9). What better rule can any of us live by than Hebrews 12:14: "Follow peace with all men, and holiness, without which no man shall see the Lord."

Today you hear many questions about what's right and what's wrong. Naturally it's impossible to have a list of rules covering everything. But the Bible does have principles that are very plain. From these we can form conclusions about specific situations. We must always go to the Bible as the real authority in matters of conduct. Don't form your convictions by what the world is saying. Unsaved people are not on God's wavelength. Their carnal reasoning is always contrary to His will.

Standards may vary from one part of the country to another. But the conscientious Christian will certainly do his utmost to avoid offending anyone. He will strive earnestly to conform his life to the teachings of the Bible.

Naturally a Christian will avoid doing anything that will negatively reflect on his testimony. If something that might seem harmless will destroy our influence with another it isn't worth it.

Above all we must refrain from anything that would bring reproach on the name of the Lord. The body of the Christian is the temple of the Holy Spirit. This means we must keep our lives clean, pure, and unspotted from the world. The Spirit of God cannot dwell where there is compromise with the principles of this age.

Think for Yourself

It's best to establish your own convictions on matters of good and evil. You can't always rely on someone else's "dos" and "don'ts." Your judgment may not be infallible, but if you sincerely try to obey the Scriptures you certainly won't get off the track.

If something interferes with your prayer life, leave it alone. If it dulls your appetite for God's Word, have nothing to do with it.

Christians can't help being different from the world. We are *supposed* to be. We are commanded in Romans 12:2: "And be not conformed to this world: but be ye transformed by the renewing of your mind, that ye may prove what is that good, and acceptable, and perfect will of God." That's holiness!

One of the greatest antidotes to yielding to temptation is staying busy for the Lord. If we fill our waking hours with service to Him we won't have nearly as many questions about right and wrong. We'll do the right thing almost automatically.

It takes time to be holy. But it's worth it.

12 No Long Faces in This Crowd!

"Be of good cheer" (John 16:33). That's Jesus speaking.

"Therefore with joy shall ye draw water out of the wells of salvation" (Isaiah 12:3). That's in the Bible too.

In fact, the Bible has so much to say about joy that the list of references would be a very long one.

Pity the person who thinks you have to be long-faced to be spiritual. Christian living brings the only kind of joy that's genuine. We aren't talking about the fleeting emotion the world calls joy. Unsaved people sometimes appear happy, but it doesn't last. Why? Because it has the wrong foundation. It depends on outward circumstances. The Christian's joy comes from within. It is not affected by what happens on the outside.

Paul named joy as one of the fruit of the Spirit (Galatians 5:22). To be joyful is the normal, natural outcome of being filled with the Spirit of God. In fact, its *un*natural for a Christian to be any other way. A happy Christian is a great testimony to the gospel.

Where Does It Come From?

We have quoted one verse from Isaiah 12. Here's the whole passage:

"And in that day thou shalt say, O Lord, I will praise thee: though thou wast angry with me, thine anger is turned away, and thou comfortedst me. Behold, God is my salvation; I will trust, and not be afraid: for the Lord Jehovah is my strength and my song; he also is become my salvation.

"Therefore with joy shall ye draw water out of the wells of salvation. And in that day shall ye say, Praise the Lord, call upon his name, declare his doings among the people, make mention that his name is exalted. Sing unto the Lord; for he hath done excellent things: this is known in all the earth. Cry out and shout, thou inhabitant of Zion: for great is the Holy One of Israel in the midst of thee" (vv. 1-6).

The source of sorrow is sin. The source of joy is freedom from sin. Isaiah is telling us in this song that sin must be confessed, but confession will be followed by thanksgiving. The process of change from the sorrow of sin to the joy of salvation is described in verse 1.

Sin brings God's anger. Only repentance and confession can change the picture. The instant God's anger is removed His favor is revealed. Remorse and guilt are gone. They are replaced with an assurance of God's acceptance. No wonder the pardoned sinner feels that salvation is a deep well from which he draws joy without ceasing.

Israel's praise book was the Book of Psalms. It abounds with expressions of joy: "Be glad in the Lord, and rejoice, ye righteous: and shout for joy, all ye that are upright in heart" (Psalm 32:11). "Make a joyful noise unto the Lord, all ye lands. Serve the Lord with gladness: come before his presence with singing" (Psalm 100:1,2). The list goes on and on.

A person out of harmony with God's will can't be truly happy. Lasting joy begins when we find Christ as our personal Saviour. That joy will continue as we live a consistent Christian life. It will deepen as we seek first the kingdom of God.

Don't be deceived at the wicked man's apparent happiness. It will be short-lived. The Bible declares in Job 20:5: "The triumphing of the wicked is short, and the joy of the hypocrite but for a moment." Worldly pleasures are glamorous for a time. Sin has a hypnotic effect. But its pleasure turns to sorrow and frustration. Today's revelry is tomorrow's weeping. God alone is the true Source of joy.

It Lasts and Lasts

Jesus' disciples were anything but happy as His crucifixion drew near. Listen to some of His teaching in those dark hours:

"These things have I spoken unto you, that my joy might remain in you, and that your joy might be full" (John 15:11).

"I will see you again, and your heart shall rejoice, and your joy no man taketh from you. . . . Hitherto have ye asked nothing in my name: ask, and ye shall receive, that your joy may be full" (16:22,24).

Jesus said His joy would "remain" in them. It would be a permanent possession. He knew His followers would face hard days. Some would be imprisoned; others would be killed. But He assured them that through all these tests His joy would never disappear from their hearts.

The world's joy is like Christmas decorations. For a few days the lights burn brilliantly. The tinsel glistens. The ornaments are a dazzle of color. But when the holiday has passed the tinsel and tree go in the trash can. The lights and ornaments are put out of sight for another year.

The so-called thrills of sinful living are the same. For a moment they give gaiety, fun, and excitement, but later there is gloom and despair. The lights go out. The fun is over.

John wrote in 1 John 1:4: "And these things write we unto you, that your joy may be full." There is nothing missing from the Christian's cup of joy. It has every necessary ingredient. It won't vanish overnight. It has the wonderful quality of permanence.

You remember how sad Jesus' disciples were before He was crucified? But what a different picture it was after His resurrection: "And they worshiped him, and returned to Jerusalem with great joy: and were continually in the temple, praising and blessing God" (Luke 24:52,53). Their joy was based on their relationship to the living Christ. That's why it lasted. Jesus promised: "Your joy no man taketh from you" (John 16:22).

In 2 Corinthians 6:10 Paul wrote: "As sorrowful, yet alway rejoicing." We may be sorely tried, but the joy of the Lord doesn't leave us. You can truthfully say this joy is the Christian's secret weapon against Satan. A happy Christian is bad news to him. It is a blow to his propaganda about all the fun you can have in sin.

The joy on the inside of a Christian will soon show itself on the outside. The world can tell it's something they don't have.

Happy Though Prosperous

Some Christians forget God during times of prosperity. It's easy to remember Him when the cupboard is almost bare. Sickness and trouble often drive us to our knees. But let's share our good times with the Lord, too. God should be uppermost in our plans when fortune smiles on us. Otherwise, those good days will become spiritually detrimental.

Israel had a feast at harvesttime. They remembered the God who had given them their good crops: "'On the three and twentieth day of the seventh month he sent the people away into their tents, glad and merry in heart for the goodness that the Lord had showed unto David, and to Solomon, and to Israel his people" (2 Chronicles 7:10).

This reminds us of Isaiah 9:3: "They joy before thee according to the joy in harvest, and as men rejoice when they divide the spoil."

Solomon had knelt before God in humble consecration at the dedication of the temple. God had prospered and blessed him and his nation greatly. Solomon recognized that God was due the praise for all these benefits. In the midst of Israel's prosperity their king led them in honoring God and giving thanks. (See 1 Kings 8.)

Job was a prosperous man. Fortunately he was the kind of man who honored God while he was prospering. There came a day when his fortunes were reversed. Not only did he lose his wealth, but also his children. Finally he lost his health. But he was able to stand the test and keep his faith in God. He wasn't like some people who "can't stand prosperity." No doubt his faithfulness in good times was the reason for his spiritual stamina in bad times.

God delights in giving His people good things. He doesn't condemn us for rejoicing when life is treating us well. All He asks is that He be allowed to share such times with us. He doesn't want us to forget to give Him thanks for all things.

Doubtless the attitude of God toward His children is expressed by John in his third epistle: "Beloved, I wish above all things that thou mayest prosper and be in health, even as thy soul prospereth" (v. 2).

If the sun is shining on your life today, thank God for it. If the clouds come you'll be able to keep on thanking Him. Thank Him for your good health, your good job, your good food—for everything.

When Things Get Tough

The depth of our joy has its real test when fortune takes the wrong turn. God's Word assures us that His joy will last through adversity as well as prosperity.

One of the greatest Biblical passages along this line is in the Old Testament. Have you ever read Habakkuk 3:17-19? Maybe you'll want to memorize it:

"Although the fig tree shall not blossom, neither shall fruit be in the vines; the labor of the olive shall fail, and the fields shall yield no meat; the flock shall be cut off from the fold, and there shall be no herd in the stalls: yet I will rejoice in the Lord, I will joy in the God of my salvation. The Lord God is my strength, and he will make my feet like hinds' feet, and he will make me to walk upon mine high places."

When Habakkuk wrote these words, the Israelites were afraid invaders were coming. If this happened

they knew the fruit trees would be destroyed, their vineyards devastated, and the olive crop ruined. Everyone was terrified at the thought. The prophet said: "When I heard, my belly trembled; my lips quivered at the voice: rottenness entered into my bones, and I trembled in myself" (v. 16).

But then something happened. The joy of the Lord broke through like the first streaks of dawn. Habakkuk shouted: "Yet I will rejoice in the Lord, I will joy in the God of my salvation." It was a cry of victory in the midst of adversity.

It is no different with us. In spite of dark times God's joy is ours. He can open the clouds and let the light shine through if we'll keep our lines of communication open to Him.

Here is a true testimony from a pioneer pastor:

"In pioneering a new church we faced many trying times. A climax was reached at one time when in the midst of a cold winter our coal supply was used up. To increase the seriousness of the situation, our food supply was gone and we had a small daughter crying for breakfast. There was no prospect for help. The outlook in the natural was grim. Somehow through it all a joy in God pervaded our hearts as we knelt to pray. Rarely had we ever sensed His joy any more than at this time.

"While we were still at prayer the telephone rang. When we answered an unknown voice asked, 'Did you get the coal?' When my wife said, 'No,' the voice continued, 'I've sent some over, and there's a box of groceries coming, too.' God had used an unsaved woman to meet our need. We learned what it meant to have joy in Him in the midst of bitter adversity."

Hang On—Victory's Coming!

The apostle Paul learned the secret of victory through trials like no other Christian who ever lived. His philosophy is beautifully expressed in Philippians 4:11-13: "Not that I speak in respect of want: for I have learned, in whatsoever state I am, therewith to be content. I know both how to be abased, and I know how to abound: every where and in all things I am instructed both to be full and to be hungry, both to abound and to suffer need. I can do all things through Christ which strengtheneth me."

Paul and his companion, Silas, spent a night in a jail at Philippi. Prisons then were terrible places of suffering and torture. But even though they were in stocks the two preachers prayed and sang at midnight. God responded with an earthquake and opened the prison doors. It pays to praise!

Enemy invasions were common for the Israelites. Second Chronicles 20 tells of such an invasion by an army much larger than Israel's. It was a day of fear and discouragement, but the people kept their faith in God. At His command, singers went out with the army. As they sang and praised the Lord, confusion struck the ranks of the enemy. The victory was Israel's. The song of joy in the hour of trial always brings help from God. "Weeping may endure for a night, but joy cometh in the morning" (Psalm 30:5).

Paul wrote to the Corinthians about a great trial experienced by the churches of Macedonia. The problems of making a living were almost insurmountable for the members of these young churches in the midst of a heathen land. In commending them, Paul wrote: "How that in a great trial of affliction, the abundance of their joy and their deep poverty abounded unto the riches of their liberality" (2 Corinthians 8:2). Their poverty was great, but so was their joy. Out of gratitude for God's help in trials they gave liberally of their meager financial means.

Joy is contagious. It has a way of overflowing and touching others. There's someone close to you who needs to feel that overflow. Just look around.

The apostle James wrote: "My brethren, count it all joy when ye fall into divers temptations" (James 1:2). We naturally feel it is better never to face tests. But James tells us to count such things a joy. Why? Because they give us an opportunity to increase our spiritual strength. They draw us closer to God and increase our trust in Him.

There's More to Come

"His lord said unto him, Well done, thou good and faithful servant: thou hast been faithful over a few things, I will make thee ruler over many things: enter thou into the joy of thy lord" (Matthew 25:21).

Fear of the future grips many today. The Christian, however, has a hope for both time and eternity. Proverbs 4:18 says it so beautifully: "But the path of the just is as the shining light, that shineth more and more unto the perfect day."

Even in this life the Christian's joy becomes deeper and more mature as time goes on. We walk with Christ a step at a time and each step is a little brighter. Our joy will reach its perfection in heaven but it gets its start right here on earth.

A happy Christian is the gospel's best advertisement. A gloomy spirit depresses our whole being, but joy is a great tonic. Let's keep drinking it in large doses! The world needs what Christ has given us.

13 Peace Without Pills

Peace! What a word! To some people it's as elusive as the will-o'-the-wisp. They have looked everywhere for it. Some have a fortune invested in their search for it.

What does peace mean to you? A good night's sleep? No worry about bills? Freedom to do exactly as you please? The only peace some people enjoy is from that little bottle they get filled at the drugstore after their doctor phones in the prescription.

Negatively, peace is the absence of war, tension, and annoyance. Positively, it is a state of calm, rest, and tranquility. Galatians 5:22 lists peace as one of the fruit of the Spirit. This is *real* peace; not the fleeting vapor that so many clutch at. It is God's gift. The more control we allow the Holy Spirit, the greater will be that peace.

The man who has peace will be a peaceable man. He will strive to avoid tension and friction with others. A person who has no peace of his own can cause all kinds of explosions. As an outlet for his own turmoil he may lash out at others.

Modern life is full of pressures. The human mind faces severe tests. Sometimes it is too much, and harrowing mental and physical experiences chew people up like a meat grinder. What are some of the by-products of this lack of peace that's so prevalent today? Marital infidelities, moral delinquencies, criminal tendencies—to name only a few. These are like wild beasts tearing at the mind. Sometimes the victims must find treatment in an institution.

Jesus Christ came to bring peace of mind to everyone who will surrender to Him. He is the Answer to the unsolvable problems that have so many backed up against a stone wall. He offers an exit from the dead-end street many a life has reached.

"Great peace have they which love thy law: and nothing shall offend them." That's God's promise in Psalm 119:165. When you really love His law you'll obey it. "Nothing shall offend them"—that means they shall have no stumbling block. They won't be forever tripping over the things that are obstacles to so many lives.

Here's another gem from the Word: "Thou wilt keep him in perfect peace, whose mind is stayed on thee: because he trusteth in thee" (Isaiah 26:3). Perfect peace—that actually means peace upon peace.

Listen, Troubled Heart!

"Therefore being justified by faith, we have peace with God through our Lord Jesus Christ" (Romans 5:1).

"Peace I leave with you, my peace I give unto you: not as the world giveth, give I unto you. Let not your heart be troubled, neither let it be afraid" (John 14:27).

"Take my yoke upon you, and learn of me; for I am meek and lowly in heart: and ye shall find rest unto your souls" (Matthew 11:29).

God's will is like a strong current. As long as we are moving in the same direction as the current we make progress. But if we try to buck the flow it's a different story. The will of God is the way of peace. Every sin a man commits takes him farther from God and, consequently, farther from peace. The first step into the perfect will of God is the forgiveness of sin.

Reconciliation—that's a great word. We read in 2 Corinthians 5:18: "And all things are of God, who hath reconciled us to himself by Jesus Christ, and hath given to us the ministry of reconciliation." That's what salvation is—God being reconciled to one who has been at war with Him.

To *reconcile* is to restore harmony between two people who have been in conflict. Have you ever heard an orchestra when the instruments were not in tune with each other? Pretty nerve-racking isn't it? The only thing to do is stop the music and get all the instruments in tune with each other. While we live in sin we're out of tune with God. So all of life is disturbed. It's one big discord. When we accept Christ we become tuned to God's will. The sour notes disappear. It's beautiful harmony now.

Remember that storm on the Sea of Galilee? Some of the disciples were fishermen, accustomed to handling boats in rough weather. As frightened as they became, you know the wind and waves had to be violent beyond description. But during all this Jesus was asleep. Probably they were too embarrassed at first to cry for help. Finally things got so bad they didn't care. Their shouts awakened Jesus. He arose serenely and spoke a word of command to the sea. Great calmness prevailed immediately.

That's what He can do for our hearts. The worst storms are the ones inside us. But when we turn to Jesus He calms them. Notice in John 14:27, He speaks of "*my* peace." A Christian's peace is supernatural. It is a gift from God. Naturally it's a mystery to the sinner. But the child of God understands.

It's Worth Searching For

God's peace doesn't fall on us from the sky while we aren't looking. First we must desire it. If it seems to elude us at first, then let us press in close to God until we find it.

"Learn of me," Jesus said. Learning is a continuous process. It goes on every day. The more we learn of Jesus, the more of His peace we will enjoy. We learn of Him through His Word and through waiting on Him in prayer. And don't forget church! New truths about our Lord come to us through worship.

What do we learn from Jesus that brings peace to our hearts? We learn that God hates sin. We discover that He is at war with every act of sin, large or small. Such knowledge leads us to realize that we will not enjoy "perfect peace" unless we live a holy life. To engage in sin of any kind is fighting against God. To shun the appearance of evil is to be marching in step with God. And that brings peace.

Jesus promised: "Ye shall *find* rest unto your souls" (Matthew 11:29). He won't let us search in vain. Rest, peace, and serenity of spirit will be ours as we follow the Lord. Times of seeming defeat will only be temporary. The gift of peace will be ours.

The Wicked Don't Have It

"But the wicked are like the troubled sea, when it cannot rest, whose waters cast up mire and dirt. There is no peace, saith my God, to the wicked" (Isaiah 57:20,21). Strong words, aren't they? But they're a perfect picture of life outside of Christ. What could symbolize restlessness better than the never-ceasing movement of the sea? If it ever seems calm you know it's temporary. Soon the waters will be boiling again. Just like the sinner's life.

This is a warning to those who would follow their sinful tendencies. They can expect the worst. Their future is bleak. The sinner is driven by his own evil impulses and passions just as the waves of the sea are driven to and fro by the wind. And as those wind-tossed waters cast up dirt and filth, so the life of the wicked casts up evil and impurity.

Is it worth it—the life of disobedience? Of course not. The evidence is everywhere. Walk up and down main street anytime and try to find faces that reflect peace. You'll find just the opposite. Tension, fear, anxiety, and apprehension is written all over the faces of rebellious souls. So is bitterness, hatred, lust, and greed. Why choose such a course? If you haven't turned from it, do it today!

Peace of Mind—Is There Such a Thing?

If you want to make some money, write a book telling people how to have peace of mind. Either the rules in such books don't work very well, or people don't practice them. Despite the multitude of pages that have tumbled off the presses, peace of mind seems an elusive goal for the majority.

But it's not an impossibility—not if you come God's way. Our world is so complicated and full of pressure it's no wonder people are disturbed. What many don't realize is that man's basic problem is spiritual. When he is adjusted spiritually, everything else will fall into its proper place.

Into our world of tension and confusion, Jesus comes to bring peace of mind. What a wonderful promise we have in Philippians 4:7: "And the peace of God, which passeth all understanding, shall keep your hearts and minds through Christ Jesus."

Let's go back to Isaiah 26:3. That "perfect peace" mentioned there comes when our mind is *stayed* on God. That means literally, "propped up." So if we want mental peace we must rest our cares on the Lord. We must prop up our mind on His grace and power.

A lot of our anxiety is of our own making. How often we borrow tomorrow's troubles. We weaken ourselves for the future by worrying so much that we are exhausted before we ever meet those troubles down the road. God's way is to trust Him a day at a time. What about the future? Leave it with Him. He can handle it a whole lot better than you or I.

What a boost it must have given Jesus' disciples when He told them: "These things I have spoken unto you, that in me ye might have peace. In the world ye shall have tribulation: but be of good cheer; I have overcome the world" (John 16:33). Did you know that the word *tribulation* literally means "pressure"? We understand that, don't we? "In the world ye shall have pressure." But Jesus said, "I have experienced the world's pressure, too. I have overcome it. Trust me, and you'll overcome too." Could anything give more peace of mind?

Sometimes peace of mind is absent because of intellectual doubts. But when you make a complete surrender to Christ He has the most wonderful way of making those doubts melt away. In their place comes a confidence in God that is unshakable. We can sing "Blessed Assurance," and really mean it. God's gift of peace comes to us through His grace. We can't earn it. Jesus earned it *for* us on the cross. And He wants us to enjoy it as long as we live.

Peace Through Forgiveness

How often the memory of past sins comes back to haunt us. This could become mental poison. But the Christian has the ministry of the Holy Spirit to rely on. How tenderly He speaks the peace of God's forgiveness to us. He reminds us that our past has been covered by the blood of Jesus Christ. How blessed is the assurance that God does not remember our sins. Our own memory of sin may not be erased, but God's peace is in our minds. It is well with our soul because God has kept His part of the bargain. We have confessed, and He has forgiven.

Overanxiety—The Enemy of Peace

Did you know that overanxiety is sin? It is an indication that we have not taken God at His Word. We are not trusting Him. Somehow we have stopped placing our confidence in His love and care.

After Jesus rose from the dead He suddenly appeared in a room where His disciples were hiding. The atmosphere crackled with anxiety. They were afraid for their lives. His first words were: "Peace be unto you" (John 20:19). Can't you imagine the change? Those frightened souls had found the cure for being uptight. Faith in their risen Saviour took care of their tension miraculously. They felt alive again.

The temptation to be overanxious is common to all of us. The Psalmist must have found the secret for an anxiety-free life, for he wrote in Psalm 4:8: "I will both lay me down in peace, and sleep: for thou, Lord, only makest me dwell in safety." Let us be conscious that God is our Heavenly Father and our days are in His hands. And our nights, too! He is concerned about us. He cares for us. He doesn't want to see us disturbed and fretful about the things that we should be turning over to Him.

Even some Christians lack peace of mind because they are too frivolous and unspiritual. We read in Romans 8:6: "To be spiritually minded is life and peace." We should seek to cultivate a spiritual mind by being filled with the Spirit, by making a constant companion of our Bible, and by a consistent prayer life. Faithful church attendance is a great help in developing spiritual-mindedness. Ours is a shallow age, and this shallowness can affect our Christian life. If it goes unchecked it can play havoc with our peace of mind. A carnal Christian shouldn't be surprised if he is plagued with overanxiety.

Prayer is always better than worry. In Philippians 4:6 Paul wrote: "Be careful [anxious] for nothing; but in every thing by prayer and supplication with thanksgiving let your requests be made known unto God."

The Bible doesn't waste words. Paul wrote about prayer and *supplication.* It takes effort to touch God. If we are careless, indifferent, or delinquent in our approach to God we will be disappointed in His response. We must move toward Him. We must desire Him. We must come as a supplicant, acknowledging our need of Him. When He sees our earnestness, peace like a river will sweep over us.

Don't Forget to Say "Thanks"

God responds to gratitude. As we think of His

past help to us let's give thanks and honor Him for meeting our needs so many times.

"Nothing so pleases God in connection with our prayer as our praise," wrote Rev. Henry Frost to a friend. The director for North America of the China Inland Mission continued: "And nothing so blesses the man who prays as the praise he offers. I got a great blessing once in China in this regard. I had received bad and sad news from home, and deep shadows had covered my soul. I prayed, but the darkness did not vanish. I summoned myself to endure, but the darkness only deepened. Just then I went to an inland mission station and saw on a wall of the mission home these words: 'Try Thanksgiving.' I did, and in a moment every shadow was gone, not to return."

It Will Make You a Better Neighbor

"If it be possible, as much as lieth in you, live peaceably with all men" (Romans 12:18).

"Let us therefore follow after the things which make for peace, and things wherewith one may edify another" (14:19).

As a Christian, your goal should be to live peaceably with everyone. It is not pleasing to God for His children to be involved constantly in quarrels and bickering. Disagreements may arise, but we should seek to settle them as graciously as possible. A Christian should cultivate a spirit of gentleness. If you go around with a chip on your shoulder, you're sure to get it knocked off!

James wrote: "But the wisdom that is from above is first pure, then *peaceable,* gentle, and easy to be entreated, full of mercy and good fruits, without partiality, and without hypocrisy" (James 3:17). This is an excellent summary of a Christian's spirit in his dealings with others. The harsh, unforgiving spirit of the world must be replaced by the peaceable, kind spirit the indwelling Holy Spirit produces.

Peace—it's wonderful!